Other books in the series:

SHIRLEY CHISHOLM

Shirley Chisholm

A Biography

SUSAN BROWNMILLER

DOUBLEDAY & COMPANY, INC.

Garden City, New York

Library of Congress Catalog Card Number 77–103736
Copyright © 1970 by Doubleday & Company, Inc.
All Rights Reserved
Printed in the United States of America

Prepared by **B** Rutledge Books
First Edition

CONTENTS

SHIRLEY CHISHOLM

CHAPTER 1

Barbados

Shirley loved her grandmother, and she loved the farm. She couldn't imagine any other kind of life. She had lived on the island of Barbados as long as she could remember. And certainly she didn't remember this Brooklyn place where she was born. It was part of New York City in the United States of America, so her grandmother told her.

Granny had told her the story often enough so that she knew it by heart. When she was three years old, she and her two sisters and four cousins had come to Barbados on a big white steamship called the *Vulcania*. Granny (Mrs. Emmeline Seales) was to look after them until their parents came to take them to Brooklyn. Her parents and her cousins' parents were working hard to save their money so one day the families could be together again. It took a long time to save the money because there was a big "depression" going on in America and jobs were

11

scarce. Jobs were particularly hard for black men to find, Shirley's grandmother told the children with an angry look in her eye. There were things called "prejudice" and "discrimination" that kept black men from good factory jobs.

But in a recent letter, which Granny had let Shirley read aloud to the other children, Shirley's mother Ruby had written that her father had gotten a new job in a burlap factory. The pay wasn't too good, but the work was steady, and the bank account—the money that they were saving to bring the children back to America—was slowly growing. "One day soon," Shirley's mother always ended her letters, "I will have my dear sweet girls here with me."

But if Shirley's mother and father were far away in America, it was still a very big family that lived together at the Seales's farm. There was Grandma Seales, Uncle Lincoln and Aunt Myrtle, and Shirley's two younger sisters. Then there were Shirley's four cousins whose mother lived in Brooklyn too.

In the early 1930s, when Shirley lived in Barbados, the tiny island was still a British colony. (Barbados was granted its independence in 1960.) Barbados is part of the group of islands known as the West Indies. Lush and fertile, the tropical islands of the West Indies appear on the map like stepping stones between the tip of Florida and the top of South America.

When Shirley looked around her she saw rolling green hills and neat square fields of sugar cane and corn. Just over the hills were the beautiful beaches of Barbados, with miles of powdered coral, both pink and white, for sand. The land was good to the Bajans (the people who lived in Barbados) and so was the sea. The local fishermen went out each morning to catch the island's specialty, the silver-glinted flying fish. The way her grandmother cooked it, flying fish was one of Shirley's favorite meals.

Shirley was a fat little girl. There were so many good things to eat on Barbados. No one ever went hungry. Even the public roads were lined with fruit-bearing trees that a little girl could climb.

When Shirley and her friends grew tired of eating fruit, they had a game that they sometimes played. They would hide in the fruit trees along the side of the road and when an unsuspecting grown-up passed by, plop, an overripe mango or pawpaw (the local name for the melonlike papaya) might just happen to fall on top of his head.

Ackee grew in pods on a pretty flowering tree that was brought to Barbados a long time ago from Africa, probably by the first black slaves that were forced to work on the island's sugar plantations in the 1600s. Because it grew on a tree, ackee was actually a fruit, but it was always cooked and eaten as a vegetable, just like another favorite of Shirley's, the green plantain, a relative of the banana. Other true vegetables that grew under the ground and that Shirley ate with chicken, pork or fish were cassava root and yams, the small delicious sweet potatoes.

Every morning Granny Seales rang a bell to call the children to breakfast. When they had eaten their hot porridge, the seven children marched together to the little schoolhouse in the village of Vauxhall. Both the younger and the older children of the village worked at their lessons from nine in the morning to four in the afternoon in the tiny one-room schoolhouse. First the village teacher would give the little children their assignment. And then, while the little ones were busy copying the alphabet onto their slates, the teacher would hold her class in arithmetic or reading for the older students.

Even the older children used slates and chalk instead of paper and pencil. The reason for this was that slates and chalk were long ago used by British children instead of pencils and paper. And many of the older British customs lingered on in the island of Barbados, long after they had died out in Britain.

Shirley learned to read in the Vauxhall classroom at the age of four. By five, she was able to copy her alphabet neatly onto her slate. At home, after dinner, she would practice her alphabet on the slate, carefully drawing her letters over and over. There was no electricity at the Seales's farm, so Shirley sat with her slate near a kerosene lamp.

Discipline in the Vauxhall village school was strict. The teacher kept a long ruler in the classroom, and she used it if the children were noisy or not paying attention. Bajans are known for their belief in a good education as the way to success in life, and the village of Vauxhall was no exception. The parents of the village always sided with the teachers, not with their children, if the children came home with a bad report from school.

"I don't want to hear any excuses," Granny Seales would say. "The teacher says you didn't know your lessons and that means you'll have to stay in the house and work on them." No pleading or begging could make her change her mind.

Shirley thrived on the discipline of school. By the age of six it was clear that she was the brightest one among her sisters and cousins. In the schoolroom she began to listen in on the older children's lessons, with the teacher's approval.

"You're a bright girl," the teacher told her one day. "Maybe when you grow up, you'll be a teacher too."

"Maybe," Shirley replied. But she couldn't really imagine what it was like to be grown up at all. She liked being a child just fine.

School and chores and homework, that was Shirley's routine during the week. But Sundays were different.

Everybody on the Seales's farm got up early on Sunday, and two at a time the children got a good scrubbing in the wooden tub in the back yard. Then Granny Seales laid out their Sunday clothes. The Sunday clothes were fresh and ironed and never worn on any other day.

Shirley and her sisters wore starched pink and yellow dresses with little round collars. Her boy cousins and Uncle Lincoln wore dark suits and black shoes. Granny herself dressed in black.

After a big Sunday breakfast—eggs and biscuits and porridge and salt fish and milk—the whole family, led by Mrs. Seales, started off on the two-mile walk to church.

Christ Church of Vauxhall Parish was a white wood building with a tall spire. It stood on top of the tallest hill in the village. It seemed to Shirley as if every road led up to that church. Just as the church bells started to ring, all the families from the nearby farms would start to walk in groups up the hill, carrying their prayer books in their hands.

Mrs. Seales led the way, followed by Uncle Lincoln and Aunt Myrtle and then the seven children. Along the way, they would meet other families that they knew, and they would give each other their special Sunday greetings, always with a formal bow.

After a lengthy session of songs and prayer, the families would start down the hill again to their homes for a Sunday dinner of chicken, fish, corn, and vegetables. Granny Seales rang her bell when the dinner was ready, and nobody ever had to be summoned a second time.

When the big Sunday meal had been consumed, the Seales family went back up the hill to Christ Church for some more singing and prayer. It was not at all unusual for Shirley and her sisters and cousins to go to church three or four times on Sunday. Everyone in the village spent most of the day at church.

As likely as not, someone Granny knew, some cousin twice removed who lived at a nearby farm, was getting married in the church on Sunday. That meant that the whole family would go to the neighbor's farm for the big wedding celebration.

Each relative would contribute a specialty to the wedding feast. One cousin would bring along a spicy pepper pot stew. Another would carry over some freshly killed chickens. Someone else would bring a basket of oranges and papaya. The parents of the bride and groom would have a large pig already roasting on an outdoor spit. Granny Seales, famous for her baking, was always asked to make a huge wedding cake with white icing. When the Seales family arrived at the wedding celebration, they couldn't help feeling proud when everyone oohed and aahed over Granny's beautiful cake.

What child wouldn't have liked Sunday on Barbados?

CHAPTER 2

Back Home to Brooklyn

When Shirley was ten, Granny Seales got an important letter. Her two daughters were coming to Barbados to take the children back to Brooklyn.

Shirley had never seen such excitement on the farm before. For two weeks, it seemed, Granny did nothing but cook and bake. One day in the kitchen Shirley saw her grandmother take a batch of rolls out of the oven. It was a new kind she had never seen before.

"Here, have one, child," her grandmother said, giving her a fresh hot bun. Shirley bit into it. It was the sweetest roll she had ever tasted. "Your mother always loved these," Granny said. Shirley looked up at her grandmother. Granny Seales was wiping a tear from her eye, Shirley was sure of it.

The smallest children didn't really understand. All they knew was that they were going to America on a big boat. Shirley had seen fishing boats in the bay, but

Granny said that the boat that was going to take her to America was much bigger than any fishing boat she had ever seen.

Shirley, Odessa, and Muriel went out back and watched as Granny took a big knife and killed one of the fattest pigs on the farm. When Granny killed a big pig, it meant they were going to have a very special feast. It all had to do with going to America.

Finally the big day arrived. Granny was up extra early, fixing things in the kitchen. The children were taken out back for the most thorough scrubbing they had ever had in their lives. Granny and Aunt Myrtle braided the girls' hair into pigtails, and then Aunt Myrtle found some ribbons in her drawer and made little bows for the braids. Shirley was given her prettiest dress to put on, a dress that she was never allowed to wear any day but Sunday.

Granny wouldn't let the children out of the house after they had dressed. "I'm not going to have you muss up your best clothes after we've gone to all this trouble getting you clean," she told them. "My daughters are going to see that I've brought their children up to be perfect ladies and gentlemen."

Shirley and her sisters and cousins sat in the house and tried to amuse themselves while they waited. Granny said that the boat that was bringing their mothers was going to land at the big pier at Bridgetown. Then their mothers would take the first public bus out of Vauxhall. The seven children waited and waited. It was the longest day Shirley had ever spent.

It was evening before they saw the bus slowly making its way up the road to the Seales's farm. The children ran out the door to meet it.

"Granny, it's here, it's here!" Shirley yelled.

"Oh my goodness, child. Lincoln, Myrtle, they're here." Grandma Seales pulled off her apron and followed the children outside.

The next hour was a confusion of hugging and crying and everybody talking at the same time.

When the families had gotten sorted out, and the mothers had said the children's names over and over, everybody moved indoors for Grandma Seales's dinner. The women hadn't eaten since breakfast on the boat, and the children had been too nervous to eat all day, so everybody—mother, child, aunt, and cousin—sat down with pleasure at the big table. Tomorrow the Seales's relatives from the neighboring village would begin to arrive to help celebrate the family reunion, but this night belonged to the children.

All through dinner Shirley couldn't keep her eyes off her mother. She was so pretty! Granny Seales was a tall, big woman. Shirley's mother by contrast was tiny.

She wore her hair parted in the middle and drawn into a low bun in the back. Shirley gaped at her mother's clothes. She had never seen anything so stylish. It was hard to believe that this small, pretty woman had grown up on the very same farm where Shirley had grown up, and was her very own mother. So that's what people in America looked like—and that's what she was going to look like too!

Mrs. St. Hill noticed her eldest daughter staring at her dress and smiled. She had made the dress herself. During the period when her husband couldn't find steady work, Shirley's mother had been able to get sewing jobs from time to time and by now she was an expert seamstress who made all her own clothes. The trunks she had brought from America were filled with clothes for the girls that she had carefully sewn by hand.

Shirley's mother and her aunt had brought five steamer trunks with them. After dinner all seven children were treated to an exciting surprise. The two mothers opened the trunks one at a time. There were American hard candies in individual cellophane wrappers for the children, and packages of chocolate cookies that everyone agreed were interesting but not quite as delicious as the cookies Grandma Seales baked.

Mrs. St. Hill had brought some new sheets and pillowcases and towels from New York for Grandma Seales.

There were some new shirts for Uncle Lincoln and a very fashionable store-bought dress for Aunt Myrtle. Each of the children got several complete new outfits, including shoes. If the shoes didn't fit one child, they did fit another, so everyone was trading gifts back and forth and admiring the wonders from America.

Each trunk held new surprises. The kerosene lamps burned very late that night at the Seales's farm. The children were allowed to stay up until the last trunk was opened and all the gifts were handed around. When Shirley finally tumbled into bed she fell right to sleep.

The next two weeks were a whirlwind of activity. Going to America, Shirley realized, was not as simple as she had thought. Her mother and her aunt made several trips into Bridgetown with all the children to get them ready for the trip.

Each child was thoroughly examined by a doctor who had to fill out forms stating that the child was in good health and not carrying a disease like mumps, measles, or chicken pox. The little ones had to have their smallpox vaccination.

Long reentry papers for the children had to be filled out by their mothers. The immigration quota for Bajans who want to live and work in the United States is very low, but since Shirley and her sisters and cousins had all been born in Brooklyn, they were already United States citizens.

Shirley liked the trips to Bridgetown. The capital city of Barbados was a colorful place. The center of Bridgetown was called Trafalgar Square. Shirley knew from her schoolbooks that there was also a Trafalgar Square in London. Bridgetown's harbor police looked just like the pictures of the British sailors in one of the books she had read. They wore white middy blouses with blue bell-bottom trousers and, on their heads, flat, wide-brimmed straw hats to protect them from the hot sun. Shirley asked if the police in New York dressed the same way and her mother and her aunt laughed.

Finally, all the children's papers were in order and it was time to go to America. The trunks were repacked with the children's clothes and sent ahead to Bridgetown by truck. The next day, Grandma Seales, Uncle Lincoln, and Aunt Myrtle rode the bus to Bridgetown with Mrs. St. Hill and her sister and the seven children.

The boat that was to take them to America was at the pier and there was no time to lose in getting aboard. Mrs. St. Hill, with Shirley, Odessa, and Muriel in tow, turned to kiss her own mother good-by.

Shirley looked up at her mother and her grandmother. Suddenly both of the women were crying. Strict, prim, upright Granny Seales had broken down completely and was wailing, "We'll never see each other again. I'll never see my daughters again. I'll never see the children again!" She was clutching at Shirley's mother and Shirley at the same time.

In one minute everyone was crying. It was a scene Shirley would never forget as long as she lived. The vivid memory of the pier in Bridgetown would stay in her mind for many years—her tall, proud grandmother wailing helplessly because she was suddenly childless.

The boat took six days to reach New York. Two of the smaller children cried for two days straight. The ocean frightened them, the boat was uncomfortably crowded, and the motion of the sea made them sick. The carefree, sunny part of Shirley's childhood was over.

The St. Hills had taken an apartment in the Brownsville section of Brooklyn on Liberty Avenue. They were one of the few black families in Brownsville at that time.

The apartment to which Ruby and Charlie St. Hill brought the children was the best that the family could afford. It was known as a cold-water flat. The apartment did have hot water, but there was no central heating. Mr. St. Hill bought a kerosene heater to try to keep the place warm, but the children, used to the tropical sun of Barbados, were miserable.

The first winter, Shirley, Odessa, and Muriel all got colds. As soon as one child got better, another would come down with a temperature. There were now four girls in the family. While Shirley and her sisters were in Barbados, the St. Hills had another baby, named Selma. Mrs. St. Hill had all she could manage that winter with baby Selma and the three girls with their colds and coughs and running noses.

It took some time for Shirley to adjust to Brooklyn. First, there was the unpleasant cold weather. Then there was the surprise of the tall buildings. Even the gray, four-story tenement buildings of Brownsville looked tall to Shirley after Barbados. In Bridgetown the buildings had been low and spaced far apart, with pretty little gardens with red hibiscus flowers surrounding them. There were few flowers in Brooklyn, and the trees did not bear fruit.

It took Shirley a while to get used to the city streets. She had never seen so much traffic, so many cars, buses, and trucks. Unlike Barbados, in Brooklyn the roadways were divided into streets and sidewalks and Mrs. St. Hill had to teach the children to walk on the sidewalks and not in the street. "You'll get hit by a car if you don't walk along close to the buildings," she told the girls.

Mrs. St. Hill had to spend most of the day in the apartment caring for baby Selma, so when she needed milk or medicine for the baby, she sent her oldest daughter to the store after school.

The drugstore was several blocks away from the apartment. Mrs. St. Hill gave Shirley careful instructions and patiently named the streets along the way. But each time Shirley went out, she forgot to look at the street signs and tried to find the way by looking for certain landmarks like the candy store and the grocery and the funeral parlor that she had noticed before and memorized. She generally got hopelessly lost. Several times a neighborhood policeman had to bring her back to the Liberty Avenue apartment.

Mrs. St. Hill would calm her upset daughter and explain once more that in Brooklyn you had to follow street signs because the stores on the street could go out of business or move to a new location on another block. Shirley was bewildered. Stores in Barbados never moved. They stayed in the same place for generations, handed down from father to son. How could a store in Brooklyn be there one week and gone the next?

That was New York City, Mrs. St. Hill explained. They were still in the depression, and people would open a store, find they didn't have enough money to keep it going, and be forced to close it down. Shirley finally memorized the street signs and stopped looking for familiar stores.

Public School 84 on Glenmore Avenue was overcrowded, so the principal had divided the schoolday into a morning shift and an afternoon shift. Shirley and her sisters got the morning shift. Two-thirds of their classmates were white.

The girls' teachers discovered that the education Shirley, Odessa, and Muriel had received in the little one-room schoolhouse in Vauxhall had been very good. After talking it over with the principal, the teachers told the St. Hill girls they were going to be skipped a grade to a more advanced class.

The girls' only problem was American history. In Barbados they had studied British history. They hadn't learned about the thirteen colonies, the Declaration of Independence, the American Revolution, and the Civil War. The sisters had to stay after school, along with some poor students who couldn't keep up with the regular work, for extra classes in American history.

Mr. St. Hill worked long hours each day at the burlap factory. His job was to pile up the big burlap bags on a loading platform for the truckmen. It was hard, backbreaking work. Shirley's father came home exhausted every night at six-fifteen. Shirley looked forward to six-fifteen each night when she would hear her father's key in the lock. It hadn't taken her long to start calling him Poppa.

As soon as Mr. St. Hill came home, Shirley's mother would begin to put the food on the table. Dinnertime was an important ritual in the St. Hill home, just as it was at Granny Seales's farm in Barbados. The whole family sat at the dinner table together. Shirley's mother and father would ask each of the girls in turn how their schoolwork had gone that day.

"I never had much of a formal education," Mr. St. Hill used to tell the children over and over. "And that's why all I can do to earn a living is work at the burlap factory. If it's the last thing I do, my girls are going to get a good education so they can do better in life than I did." Mrs. St. Hill always agreed with her husband.

At the farm in Barbados, Granny had always been strict about the children doing the chores. But Shirley's mother never pushed the children much to help her around the house. She was strict about their homework though. "Your job is to study," she always told them. "Bring home a good report card and that will be enough for me. I can manage the household chores. You tend to your studying."

Mrs. St. Hill was worried about all the colds that the girls caught every winter. At last she told her husband that she was going to search for a steam-heated apartment. She finally found one on Ralph Avenue in the Bedford-Stuyvesant section of Brooklyn.

Shirley and her sisters were transferred to P.S. 28 on Herkimer Street. The teachers at the new school were so impressed with Shirley's ability that they skipped her again.

The problem with the Ralph Avenue apartment was that the rent was more than Mr. St. Hill could manage. Jobs were still scarce and the pay was very low at the factory. Because so many people were unemployed there was no chance of earning extra money with overtime. When Selma was old enough to go to school, Mrs. St. Hill decided to earn the extra money they needed by working a few days a week.

Shirley's mother found day work as a maid in the Flatbush section of Brooklyn. She cleaned, did washing and ironing, and scrubbed floors for forty cents an hour plus carfare.

On the days when Shirley's mother had to go to work, she laid the children's lunch out on the table before she left in the morning. Mrs. St. Hill put Shirley in charge of the younger children. She had an extra key made for the door, and put it on a piece of string that she tied around Shirley's neck. "That way you won't lose it," she told Shirley.

At the noon recess from school, Shirley picked up Odessa, Muriel, and Selma at their classrooms and brought them home to the Ralph Avenue apartment for lunch, carefully using the key around her neck to open the door.

Shirley took her new responsibility very seriously. Odessa and Muriel used to complain that she was too strict with them about finishing their food, but Shirley made sure they ate everything on their plates. Her mother had told her she was in charge. After lunch she would walk them back to school.

Most of the black children in the neighborhood had mothers who had to work as cleaning women in other people's houses to make ends meet in their own homes. All the older children wore the telltale keys around their necks on strings. Shirley and the others were known in the neighborhood as the "latch-key children."

Now in the evening Shirley's father and her mother both came home tired and worn. Sometimes Mrs. St. Hill walked into the house with a shopping bag. In it were castoff clothing and leftover food from the families she worked for. The leftovers became part of the evening meal Mrs. St. Hill served to her family.

Shirley hated to see her mother grow so worn before her eyes. All the prettiness had gone from Mrs. St. Hill's face and in its place was a hard look of bitter determination.

Mrs. St. Hill told her husband she wanted to move again. At night after Shirley had gone to bed she could hear her mother and father arguing in the kitchen. "I want my girls to have their own bedroom," Mrs. St. Hill was saying. "They're growing up and they need some privacy."

"You know we can't afford a larger place, Ruby," Mr. St. Hill answered in a low voice. "I could be laid off at any time at the factory and we're barely managing to keep our heads above water now."

"My girls are going to have their own beds in their own bedroom," Mrs. St. Hill replied. "I'll find us an apartment somewhere. You'll see."

Mrs. St. Hill was true to her word. She did find a larger apartment. The landlord agreed to rent it to her at a reduced price when Mrs. St. Hill said she would do all the janitor work in the building. So the family packed up all its belongings and moved again.

The new apartment was on Patchen Avenue. There was plenty of room for the girls. Mrs. St. Hill kept up her share of the bargain with the landlord by tending to the coal furnace and putting the heavy garbage cans out in front early in the morning for the sanitation trucks to take away. Once a week she mopped the hallways and the staircases of the building from top to bottom.

Shirley watched her mother and understood. "She's doing this for my sisters and me," Shirley said to herself. "I'd better not disappoint her."

CHAPTER 3

Three Heroines

Shirley went to Junior High School 178 on Herkimer and Saratoga and then on to Girls' High. She was beginning to have a social life. She and her sisters loved to go to parties where there was dancing.

Shirley discovered that she was very good at dancing. Sometimes when she and her partner were on the dance floor the others would gather around and clap their hands and watch.

"It's funny," she thought, "how I seem to come alive on the dance floor. I know just what to do with my hands and body. I just have to see a step once and I can do it."

A dance called the lindy was popular at the time, and Shirley mastered the steps easily. Her friends would buy some records and they would all get together at each other's homes and lindy and jitterbug. Shirley's favorite dances, she soon discovered, were the Latin ones, especially the rumba and the conga. The whole nation seemed to be in a Latin music craze just then and Shirley was no exception. She could rumba all night, making up her own steps as she went along.

Mrs. St. Hill was horrified by her teen-age daughters' new craze for dancing. "Where will it all lead?" she would say sternly to Shirley and her sisters. "All this fooling around with the boys at your parties will get you into trouble. No nice girl would do those wild dances."

Shirley and her sisters tried to argue that all American teen-agers danced to records, but Mrs. St. Hill wouldn't listen. Rumba-ing and conga-ing was not the way she was brought up in Barbados.

"If the children like music so much," Mrs. St. Hill told her husband one evening, "I think I'll get them a piano. Maybe that will get them off the wild dancing."

Mr. St. Hill just smiled. He had learned long ago that when his wife got something on her mind, there was no stopping her until it was accomplished.

Sure enough, it was just a matter of time before Mrs. St. Hill had purchased a secondhand piano and had it hauled up into the apartment through a window. Shirley did like playing the piano, as it turned out. She spent many pleasant hours practicing. But the piano didn't stop her from dancing. She had a lot of energy to get rid of, and dancing was the best way to do it. Besides, she was so good at dancing now that she had even won some prizes at local dance competitions, and winning was a very good feeling.

Mrs. St. Hill particularly disapproved of the big dances the girls loved to go to—the ones that the local boys' social clubs would hold on Saturday nights. When the St. Hill girls were invited to a Saturday night dance, they were allowed to go only if they promised to be home before midnight. "Mother must think we're little Cinderellas," Shirley said to her sisters.

It always happened that Shirley was on the dance floor with her favorite partner when her sister Muriel came rushing over to point frantically at her watch. Shirley never got over being embarrassed that the St. Hill girls were always the first to leave every party. "We must be the laughingstock of the neighborhood," she told Muriel as the girls walked home from a dance one night.

Shirley never let her prizes at the dance competitions turn her away from her first love, reading. Ever since the days of Granny Seales's farm, when she had read her schoolbooks far into the night by the light of a kerosene lamp, Shirley had adored all kinds of books. She was a fast reader, sometimes going through a book a night. Often the mention of an interesting-sounding person in her American history class would send her to the library to learn more about that person. Since those early days when she had to stay after school to do extra work, Shirley had become a serious student of American history. She was fascinated by the lives of those who influenced the course of American politics.

The lives of three people especially interested her. Not surprisingly, all three were women. They had one other quality in common: they were fighters. The three women that the teen-age Shirley most admired were Harriet Tubman, Susan B. Anthony, and Mary McLeod Bethune.

In the life story of Harriet Tubman, Shirley discovered an important chapter in American history that was only touched upon in her classes. Harriet Tubman, herself an escaped slave from a Maryland plantation, repeatedly risked danger and death to bring slaves North to freedom during the years before the Civil War.

Shirley felt that there was nobody else like Harriet Tubman in American history. The tiny, tough black woman always carried a pistol on her trips down South to the slave plantations. The pistol was for use against betrayers or slave hunters, but Harriet Tubman never had to use it. She was too clever. The slave hunters could never catch her, and none of her own people ever betrayed her.

Dressed in men's clothes to be less conspicuous, Harriet would arrive at a plantation under the cover of night. When she got within shouting distance of the plantation, she sang a song that the slaves knew—like "Follow the Drinking Gourd"—to reveal her presence to those who were expecting her. She led her parties of escaped slaves through woods and swamps to the free states of the North by following the North Star in the sky—the "Drinking Gourd" was a code for the stars that formed the Big Dipper which pointed to the bright North Star.

When she got her parties of escaped slaves up North, Harriet would take them to the homes of freed black men and white abolitionists for sleep and food. That was the Underground Railroad, the secret network of friends and sympathizers that "conductors" like Harriet Tubman relied on.

Harriet Tubman's reputation became legend in the South. Her code name was Moses. The white slaveholders put a price on her head. They wanted her captured, dead or alive. But the slaveholders couldn't believe that "Moses" was a woman. One slaveholder even offered a reward of $40,000 for the capture of "the escaped male slave known as Moses."

Shirley devoured every scrap of information about Harriet Tubman. She learned that Harriet fought as a soldier in the Union Army during the Civil War. She led a troop of three hundred Negro soldiers in one of the most successful raids of the war—against the Confederate forces in South Carolina.

Shirley also learned, with bitterness, that after the war, the U. S. Government for many years denied Harriet Tubman a soldier's pension, to which she was entitled, because she was black and a woman.

One day in school, a white boy in Shirley's class had insulted her. They were comparing grades on their test papers. Shirley had gotten the higher mark, and the boy had said, "When I graduate from high school I'm going on to college, but I guess you're not. Negroes don't go to college, do they?"

Shirley had burned. Stiffly she told him that her mother and father expected all four of their children to go to college, and that since her grades were always higher than his, she would have an easier time getting into college too.

The boy was taken aback by Shirley's fast answer, but he wouldn't let the conversation drop. "So what if you get good marks," he went on. "It's much more important for a boy to go to college than a girl. Girls never do anything. They just become housewives. When I grow up I can be President of the United States."

"This girl is going to do something when she grows up," Shirley shot back.

"Oh yeah?"

"Yeah. Or rather, *yes*. My mother taught me to say yes, not yeah. I guess your mother never taught you manners." That ended the argument, and Shirley felt she had won it, but the things the boy had said to her bothered her more than she cared to admit to him.

She knew her American history well enough to know that no black man and no woman—black or white—had ever been elected President. "Why *not?*" she said to herself. "Why *not?*" The girls in her class were just as bright as the boys, and some were even brighter. Why didn't the country let them use their intelligence and education to the fullest?

Was it because, as some people hinted, that women didn't want to make anything of themselves? It couldn't be that, Shirley reasoned. That's what people used to say about Negroes. But Shirley knew that white people had always kept black people down. So it must be, she said to herself, that men also wanted to keep women from getting ahead—maybe to keep the good jobs for themselves.

Shirley's second favorite heroine, after Harriet Tubman, was Susan B. Anthony. She was a white woman who spent her life fighting for equality for women. Susan Anthony and Harriet Tubman, Shirley discovered through her reading, were born in the same year, 1820. Harriet was born a slave in Maryland. Susan was born to middle-class Quaker parents on a farm in Massachusetts.

In those days in America, women were not allowed to vote or even hold property in their own name. Women who dared to speak out openly and demand a change in the laws were publicly laughed at.

Susan and a few other women organized a powerful women's rights movement by holding meetings and lectures across the United States. Susan even published a weekly newspaper for women's rights. She called it *The Revolution.*

When the women's rights movement first began, few women or men came to listen to Susan B. Anthony speak. And sometimes when they did come, there were riots. But she went on handing out leaflets, collecting signatures on petitions, and organizing meetings in public halls. She developed a lecture called "Bread and the Ballot." It was a ringing plea to give women the vote to better their economic conditions.

Once, as a test case, Susan marched to the polls and actually voted along with her three sisters in the town of Rochester, New York. She was arrested and found guilty and fined in a court trial. The jurors were all men, of course. *Women* weren't even allowed to serve on a jury—as blacks, men or women, were not allowed to serve on a jury down South.

For a few years before the Civil War Susan B. Anthony devoted herself full-time to the antislavery cause.

Harriet Tubman once deposited an escaped slave at Susan's house in Rochester for food and clothing before taking the fugitive farther on the Underground Railroad to Canada and freedom. Susan and Harriet often shared the same speaker's platform at women's suffrage and abolition meetings.

There was much in the lives of Susan B. Anthony and Harriet Tubman that the young Shirley could identify with. It made her dizzy to think of such powerful, independent women who by organization, speeches, and courageous action overcame fearful odds and helped to change the course of events of the nation.

If Susan and Harriet could do it, why couldn't she? Anything was possible, wasn't it?

Shirley looked around her for examples of modern women who had the courage of Harriet and Susan. All the boys she knew, and most of the girls, had found their hero in Joe Louis, the heavyweight champion of the world. The Brown Bomber, as Joe Louis was called, *was* inspiring. He could lick any man in the world with his boxing gloves. On the night of a Joe Louis fight, everyone she knew sat glued to the radio, waiting for Joe's knockout punch. And Joe seldom disappointed them.

Shirley was as overjoyed as anyone when Joe Louis won a fight. But, she told herself with a laugh, the one thing she certainly wasn't going to grow up to be was a heavyweight boxing champion of the world!

Shirley found her third heroine in Mary McLeod Bethune. Mrs. Bethune was a trusted friend and adviser of President Franklin Delano Roosevelt when Shirley first became aware of her existence.

The fifteenth child of parents who had been born slaves, the young Mary McLeod had grown up on a farm in South Carolina. She had gotten her first schooling at the age of eight at a Presbyterian mission school. In the early years after Emancipation it was still rare for black children to be sent to school and young Mary had to endure the taunts of white children who made fun of her for wanting to learn.

Learn she did, and education became the guiding force of her life. When still a young woman, she founded a school for Negro girls in Daytona, Florida, getting the black and white community to support her effort by cake sales, fund-raising suppers and pleas to sympathetic businessmen for financial support. The school later became known as Bethune-Cookman College and it took in young men as well as young women.

When Shirley was going to high school, she often saw Mrs. Bethune's picture in the newspaper, as the founder and president of the National Council of Negro Women, as a vice-president of the NAACP—the National Association for the Advancement of Colored People—as a special adviser to President Roosevelt for minority affairs, and as the director of the Division of Negro Affairs for the National Youth Administration.

Shirley liked to see the newspaper photos of Mrs. Bethune with Eleanor Roosevelt, the President's politically active wife. And she liked the group pictures of President Roosevelt and his aides with Mrs. Bethune standing tall and proud among them.

And she especially liked the dignity of this stately black woman. Her name even sounded majestic. Mary McLeod Bethune—it had an important ring to it. Shirley wondered if she would ever be photographed with the President of the United States.

CHAPTER 4

To College—On Scholarship

Shirley tore open the important-looking white envelope. "A scholarship to Barnard College," she told her mother proudly. "And last week I got an offer of one to Hofstra."

Mrs. St. Hill looked at the letter. "That's the fourth scholarship you've been offered, isn't it? I knew my daughter was bright, but I never dreamed that the colleges would pay her money to go to their schools. Have you decided which offer you'll accept?"

"I think," Shirley said slowly, "that I'm going to go to Brooklyn College. These scholarships will pay for my tuition, but if I go to Brooklyn, the tuition is free, anyhow. I can live at home and save money on living expenses too. Those other two scholarships I got can be used at Brooklyn College, and they'll more than pay for my books and supplies. Brooklyn has a good academic standing. What more could I want?"

"Some of your friends are going to Brooklyn, too, aren't they?" Mrs. St. Hill asked.

"The ones who passed the entrance exams," Shirley laughed. "That two-day examination for Brooklyn College was the hardest exam I ever took."

Shirley started Brooklyn College that fall, the first member of her family to get a higher education. The Brooklyn College campus was right in the heart of Flatbush, the neighborhood where Shirley's mother had worked as a domestic a few years before.

Shirley liked Brooklyn's campus. The low, red brick buildings with white wood trim had a pleasant colonial look to them, and they faced on a large grass square. The grass on the square—the students called it the quadrangle—was always trim and neat. The campus even had a small bridge and a tiny water lily pond, with benches alongside it that made a comfortable, quiet spot for reading between classes. For socializing, there was the noisy basement cafeteria, where the students gathered with their trays of food and compared classroom lecture notes about politics.

The slim, dark, intense young woman with glasses who hurried to and from her classes on the quadrangle was a far cry from the fat little girl who loved to run barefoot on the island of Barbados.

Shirley decided to major in sociology at Brooklyn.

She showed her parents the college catalogue where the different courses were listed. "You see," she explained to them, "sociology will teach me how different groups of people behave among themselves and how they relate to society. I've always been interested in the relationship between black and white and rich and poor in this city, and that's what sociology is all about."

"How does sociology train you to earn a living, Shirley?" her father asked.

"It's a good background for a lot of things," Shirley answered. "If I decide to go into teaching, and I probably will, sociology is a fine major to have. And it's also the best thing if I go into social work. Whatever I do with my life, I'm sure it will have something to do with helping others, and sociology will help me to understand a lot about the world."

"The world needs a lot of help right now," Shirley's mother said.

"You can say that again," said Mr. St. Hill as he went to switch on the radio. "Let's listen to the news."

Every night the St. Hills listened to the news about the Second World War, which was raging in Europe and the Pacific. Many young men that the St. Hills knew in the neighborhood had been drafted to fight overseas. In Shirley's Brooklyn College class, the only male students left were the ones that the draft board had classified 4-F.

The St. Hills, like all other American families, helped with the war effort on the home front. Shirley and her sisters saved rubber bands and tin foil, which the neighborhood boys came around weekly to collect. Mrs. St. Hill poured her used cooking fat into jars and took it to her butcher once a week. President Roosevelt had announced on the radio that the tin foil, rubber bands, and fat were needed for the war effort.

There was a food shortage in America during World War II. There was never enough coffee, sugar, or meat to go around. Each family was given ration books with little stamps, and Mrs. St. Hill had to use the stamps when she did her grocery shopping. The storekeepers wouldn't sell Shirley's mother sugar or meat or coffee or many other things unless she gave them stamps from the ration book. Several of Mrs. St. Hill's neighbors got together and set up a Victory garden where they grew their own vegetables.

Shirley threw herself with determination into her studies at Brooklyn College. After the first term she discovered that the work was going to be no problem—she was doing well, just as she had always done well at school. Finding she still had energy to spare, she looked around and joined a few clubs that met on campus after classes.

To her surprise and joy, she found that Brooklyn College had a Harriet Tubman Society. Shirley promptly became an active member. In those days at Brooklyn College the local sororities, known as "house plans," did not admit Negroes to membership, and the Harriet Tubman Society brought the issue of the discriminating sororities to the attention of the campus at large.

Shirley had never been shy about speaking up in school, despite some difficulty pronouncing her "S's," and one thing she discovered about herself was that she loved to argue a political point. Brooklyn College had a Debating Society, and Shirley decided to attend a couple of its meetings. Before she knew it, the Debating Society became her favorite after-class club.

Shirley and her teammates argued such questions as whether "the U. S. Armed Forces Should Be Integrated"; whether "The United States Should Abolish Capital Punishment"; or whether "The Poll Tax in the South Should Be Abolished." Whenever a hot issue was in the news, the Debating Society examined both sides and presented the arguments.

Shirley discovered she was turning into a fiery speaker who could stand up on her two feet and talk with just a page of notes and facts to guide her. She loved to be the captain and "cleanup" speaker for her team, the one who spoke last and summed up all the facts for her side.

"I can really persuade people when I speak," she thought. "And I'm getting better at it all the time. It's a good feeling to be able to move people with words, to convince them with facts and a clearly presented argument."

The test, of course, was when the club members voted on which side had presented the better arguments and had won the debate. Shirley's team didn't always win, but it won more often than it lost.

Professor Louis Warsoff of the political science department often came to the Debating Society meetings to hear the students conduct their debates. Once, when Shirley's team was arguing whether "Eighteen Year Olds Should Be Allowed to Vote," Professor Warsoff came over to Shirley after the debate and congratulated her on her presentation.

On another occasion, when Shirley was serving as moderator between the two sides, Professor Warsoff made a special point of telling her how well she had handled herself.

"You were able to see both sides of the issue," the professor told her, "and your questions to the debaters were right to the point. You brought up interesting side issues that they had missed." Shirley felt flattered and very pleased.

One day in her senior year, Professor Warsoff called

Shirley into his office. "Well, Miss St. Hill, how's our champion debater?" he asked.

"Very well, thank you," Shirley answered. She wondered why Professor Warsoff had asked to speak to her. She wasn't taking any classes with him this year, so it couldn't be that there was something wrong with her grades.

The professor came right to the point. "Have you thought about what you're going to do after you graduate, Shirley?" he asked.

"I'll probably teach for a living," Shirley answered a bit stiffly. "It's an area that's open to Negro women, as you know, and it's something I think I'd do well. My early education in Barbados was excellent, and I think that's what prepared me to do well in school later on. I'd like to help other children the way I was helped to learn to read and write."

"Yes, I think you would make a good teacher," Professor Warsoff replied. "But I wonder if you'll find the teaching profession challenging enough. You're a young woman with a lot of energy and a very scrappy personality, and you're obviously quite concerned with social issues." Professor Warsoff paused before he went on. "I wonder if you've ever thought of going into politics."

"Politics?" Shirley's voice was raised a full octave.

"Yes. Does the idea surprise you? I happen to think

you're a natural for it. I think you might be able to make quite a contribution in the political field."

Shirley shook her head in disbelief. The only black woman she had ever heard of in politics was Mary McLeod Bethune, but even Mrs. Bethune wasn't really in politics—she was an educator to whom President Roosevelt gave important government assignments. What in the world was Professor Warsoff driving at?

Shirley thought back to the white boy in her public school class who had said "Negroes don't go to college" and "Girls don't do anything important in life." But Professor Warsoff was white, too, and he was looking at her very seriously. He certainly wasn't making fun of her.

"Professor Warsoff," Shirley began formally, "I'm black and a woman. How many black women do you know of in politics? How many black women are there in the United States Congress?"

"None," the professor answered, lighting his pipe. "But there's got to be a first sometime, don't you think? And if there's got to be a first, I think you'd be the right person. Frankly, I think you're the sort of person who wouldn't settle for anything else."

Shirley was speechless. She seldom confided her hopes and ambitions to anyone, and here was this white man, a college professor, who was talking to her about her future and describing goals far greater than those she usually allowed herself to dream about.

"Professor Warsoff," Shirley said slowly, "I may not know much about practical politics, but from what I do know, I'd say that on the local level it's pretty corrupt. Negroes aren't even allowed to become members of the local Democratic clubs in Brooklyn."

"That will change," Professor Warsoff said serenely. "And you can be one of the people who make it change."

"Well, what could I do?" Shirley said in a small voice, conscious that what she had just asked wasn't a very sophisticated question.

"I'm not suggesting that you go out tomorrow and run for Congress," Professor Warsoff laughed. "You have plenty of time. What I suggest is that you involve yourself on a local level, in your community. That's the way a real politician begins—right in his own neighborhood, helping people with their problems. What do you see as the major problems in your own neighborhood?"

"Bad housing . . . discrimination . . . poor jobs with no chance of advancement."

"See what I mean?" Professor Warsoff said triumphantly. "You hit the nail right on the head, as you usually do. The first step is to recognize the problems, the second step is to begin to do something about them. My advice to you is to work in your own neighborhood

53

to correct some of those wrongs you just mentioned. Apply that mind of yours, use that energy and that gift of speech you have, and begin to organize."

"Organize?"

"Well, you can't do it all by yourself. No one is going to listen just to you. You have to get people together and build an organization of neighborhood people who are willing to fight to change those conditions—the bad housing, the discrimination, and the poor jobs. That's what politics is all about. I'm not talking about corrupt politics. I'm talking about the kind of politics that brings about change."

Shirley thought about Susan B. Anthony and Harriet Tubman. Yes, that's what Professor Warsoff was talking about. But he wasn't talking about American *history*, he was talking about the present—and the future, and her role in it.

Shirley left the professor's office with her head spinning. Politics! Would she ever dare?

CHAPTER 5

"Jamaican Men Always Want the Best"

Shirley graduated from Brooklyn College in 1946. The war had been over for one year. Mr. St. Hill had managed during the war years to save a sizable amount of money for the first time in his life because of overtime work at the factory. He put down $10,000 on a fine three-story brick row house on Prospect Place on the edge of Bedford-Stuyvesant. The St. Hills became homeowners in Brooklyn at last!

Mrs. St. Hill was overjoyed. The house had a full basement and a garden out in front, and there was an imposing flight of concrete steps leading up to the front door. It was a world away from the cold, steamless, overcrowded tenement apartment that she had taken her daughters to when they came from Barbados in 1934.

Shirley had little time to spend at the new house, however. And for the time being she had to put aside Professor Warsoff's ideas and suggestions for the future. For the moment, Shirley had enough to do—she had to get a job, earn her living. And, at the same time, she knew she wanted to get further training. Politics—and the challenge of that sort of work, which Shirley knew she would enjoy—would have to wait.

Early each morning Shirley took the subway train up to Harlem where she had found a job as a nursery school teacher at the Mount Calvary Child Care Center. After her day's work with the children, she barely had time for a quick bite to eat before she took the train farther uptown to Washington Heights and Columbia University. To improve her skills, she enrolled in the evening classes at Columbia's School of Education, working for a master's degree.

After her evening classes at Columbia, she got back on the train for the ride back to Brooklyn each night. The long train rides each day were tiring, but Shirley got into the habit of opening her books and studying on the train, unmindful of the other passengers.

The schedule Shirley set up for herself—rushing from job to school and then back home again to sleep—was a rugged one. It left her no time for a social life. She planned her weekends so she could devote most of her time to studying. But she still loved to dance, and once in a great while she would take time to go dancing.

At one of those rare Saturday night dances that

Shirley allowed herself to attend, she was introduced by friends to a pipe-smoking, solidly built young graduate student from Jamaica named Conrad Chisholm. They chatted for a while between dances, and before she knew it, Shirley was telling Conrad about her job with the children at the Harlem nursery. He seemed interested in what she had to say, so Shirley went on and described to him the classes she was taking at Columbia.

The young man suddenly broke into her monologue. "Don't you ever stop to have any fun?" he asked gently.

Shirley was taken aback. "That's a rather fresh question," she retorted. "I happen to enjoy my work, and I love going to Columbia."

"There are other things in life besides work and school," Conrad replied with a twinkle in his eye. "How about having dinner with me one night this week?"

"I never take time off during the week for socializing," Shirley said rather primly. "I can't afford to fall behind in my studies." She was sorry she was being so stand-offish with this nice young man from Jamaica with his soft, lilting accent, but he didn't look the sort of fellow who would have difficulty finding some other young lady to take out to dinner.

To her surprise, Conrad Chisholm refused to take no for an answer. "I happen to know a good Jamaican restaurant that I think you'd like," he went on with a confident smile.

"You Jamaican men are pretty sure of yourselves, aren't you?" Shirley said with a laugh. She was beginning to enjoy sparring with this fellow.

"Jamaican men always want the best," Conrad Chisholm replied. "And I'm going to take you out to dinner."

He did just that. The two spent a long evening discussing the relative merits of Barbados and Jamaica. As West Indians, Conrad and Shirley discovered that they had a lot in common. The conversation never seemed to run out.

"Who is this man who can upset my vital day-to-day plans?" Shirley asked herself that night after Conrad had taken her home. "Could he become important to me?"

He could. A year later they were married. Shirley was twenty-five years old. One of the first things she did was to get some stationery printed up with her new name, Shirley Chisholm. She like the sound of it, and she liked the way it looked printed on the paper.

"You always said Jamaican men want the best," Shirley told her husband. "So you just *had* to marry a Bajan girl."

Conrad and Shirley rented a small house in Brooklyn not far from Shirley's parents. Shirley, her master's degree from Columbia under her belt, was appointed director of a private nursery school in Brownsville.

"See," she told Conrad gaily. "No more long subway rides for me. When you first met me all I did, it seemed, was ride the subways morning and night."

"Somehow I can't imagine my wife not on the move," Conrad answered. Shirley glowed. Her husband always knew just what to say to her. His calm personality was a wonderful foil for her excitable nature. Whenever anything went wrong at the nursery, and Shirley come home upset, she would talk it over with Conrad, who always managed to cheer her up.

Yes, Conrad was an unusual man, Shirley thought. She couldn't imagine being married to anyone else. Some of her girl friends had husbands who didn't want their wives to have any independent life at all. They were actually jealous of their wives' careers. But Conrad understood that a career of her own was important to *his* wife, and he always encouraged her to do her best.

Shirley decided that one of the reasons why her husband was different was that Conrad was deeply involved with his own job, which he thoroughly enjoyed. Conrad Chisholm had gone into private detective work shortly after he met Shirley. When he told Shirley about some of the cases he was investigating, they sounded as exciting as anything out of a detective story.

Conrad's reputation as a private investigator was growing and he was offered a good job doing investigation work for a big railroad company. He came home and discussed the offer with Shirley.

"It sounds like a good job," he said, drawing on his pipe. "I'll be working on cases of railroad men who claim they were injured on the job, and who are suing the railroad company for damages. My job will be to determine if they really are injured, and how seriously, without letting them know, of course, that I represent the railroad. Some of these men fake their injuries and then try to sue the company for a quarter of a million dollars. It will be tricky work—getting them to talk to me, talking to their neighbors, things like that, without letting them know that I'm really investigating them."

"So far, so good," Shirley said. "Why are you hesitating?"

"Well, the railroad company told me I'd be traveling a lot. They'd be sending me to places like Chicago. When I'm on a case, it might take more than two weeks to get all the facts for my report. That means that I'll be away from home for long periods of time. How do you feel about that?"

"I won't like it, certainly. But I think the job sounds too good to turn down."

"Good. That's what I hoped you'd say." Conrad

smiled broadly. "We must promise each other that one of us will never interfere with the other's career."

"And always help each other to the best of our ability," Shirley added.

"It's a deal."

Shirley did miss Conrad when he was away from home, but soon she had an important new job to keep her busy. She was appointed director of the Hamilton-Madison Child Care Center on the Lower East Side of Manhattan.

The Hamilton-Madison Center was located right in the middle of a huge housing project. Shirley had more than 150 black and Puerto Rican children who came to the nursery each day. Working under her were several assistant teachers and social workers.

When Conrad came home from his trips, Shirley would fill him in on what had gone on that week at the center. "The Puerto Rican children are adorable—they're teaching me Spanish," she told her husband at one point. "They teach me Spanish and I teach them English. We have no trouble communicating at all. Actually, my only problems are with some of the social workers. Their ideas on education and mine are somewhat different."

"What do you mean?" Conrad asked his wife.

"Well, I think that the children should be on a strict

schedule. They should take their naps at a certain hour, get up at a certain hour, and even have their milk and cookies at a certain hour each day. I have some people working for me who don't care about schedules at all. Now, when I was growing up in Barbados, Granny was very strict with us children. We were sent to school at age three and a half. It worked for me, and I think it would work for these children too."

"Do you tell that to the social workers?" Conrad asked.

"Oh yes," Shirley laughed. "I call staff meetings all the time, and we have very interesting discussions. I'm in charge and they know it, so they're coming around to doing things my way."

"You sound like a tough boss, Shirley," Conrad said to his wife. He smiled. "Now forget your problems and let me tell you what happened to me this week in Chicago."

After a half hour of listening to Conrad, Shirley felt totally relaxed. She forgot about the problems at Hamilton-Madison Child Care Center.

The evenings were the difficult part of Shirley's life when Conrad was away on the road, although he always remembered to keep in touch with her by telephone. She wasn't the sort of person who could sit quietly at home watching television, and there were just so many books a person could read in one week.

Something was stirring in her neighborhood of Bedford-Stuyvesant, and Shirley got wind of it. In 1953 a local Negro lawyer named Lewis Flagg decided to run for judge in the next election. The white bosses who controlled Brooklyn's Democratic Party machine brought in a white lawyer from outside the neighborhood as their candidate for the judgeship.

"Isn't that just like those corrupt politicians," Shirley told Conrad on the telephone one night. "Bedford-Stuyvesant is now an almost all-black neighborhood, and those politicians won't let a black man get the job."

"Does Flagg have any organization working for him?" Conrad asked.

"I hear there's something called the Bedford-Stuyvesant Political League," Shirley answered. "They've opened up a headquarters in an empty store in the neighborhood. I passed it on the way to the subway this morning."

"Why don't you go down and look into it?" Conrad suggested. "They probably need someone with your organizing abilities."

"Maybe you're right," Shirley replied. "It just makes me mad the way these white politicians act so high-handed."

The following evening, Shirley walked over to the store front where the Bedford-Stuyvesant Political League was located. She asked who was in charge, and was introduced to a tall and courtly black man named Wesley Holder.

Holder wasted no time in asking Shirley if she was a registered Democrat. When she told him she was, he asked if she had signed a nominating petition for Lewis Flagg. Shirley hadn't, but she promptly signed the petition when Holder presented it to her.

"Do you know if your friends and neighbors are registered Democrats, Mrs. Chisholm?" Holder asked.

"I'm pretty sure my friends are all registered voters," Shirley replied. "I don't know if they're all Democrats."

"Would you like to take a nominating petition home with you and ask your friends to sign for Lewis Flagg? The only way we can get him on the ballot is if we have enough signatures. Since Mr. Flagg is running in the Democratic primary, all the signers must be registered Democrats."

Shirley took the nominating petition home with her. She liked this Wesley Holder. He struck her as a shrewd person who knew what he was doing. She smiled to herself. "I'm getting mixed up in politics," she thought. "Sort of edging in. Professor Warsoff was right."

Two evenings later, Shirley walked into the League's

headquarters with fifteen signatures on the nominating petition Holder had given her.

"It wasn't as easy as I thought it would be," Shirley told Holder. "I had to ring a lot of doorbells to get these fifteen signatures. Some people whom I just assumed were registered voters turned out not to be registered at all. And some of those who were registered said we were crazy—that a black man would never get to be a judge in Brooklyn."

"That's our problem, Mrs. Chisholm," Holder told her. "Most of the black people in this neighborhood are not registered to vote, and many of the others don't think we stand a chance. One of our jobs will be to get hundreds of new people registered so they can vote for Flagg in the general election. I know we can do it, and I hope you'll continue to help us."

Shirley nodded. "Give me another one of those nominating petitions," she said suddenly. "I just thought of some more people I can ask to sign."

Holder looked at Shirley with surprise. "When you take on a project, Mrs. Chisholm, you really work at it, don't you?" he said.

"That's how I approach everything in life, Mr. Holder," Shirley replied. "And I like to be on the winning team."

Shirley and Wesley Holder grew to be good friends

during the Flagg campaign. Shirley liked the well-mannered politician from British Guiana, and he, in turn, gave her more and more responsibility as the campaign wore on. The campaign was a bitter one, but when it was over, Lewis Flagg had been elected judge.

Shirley Chisholm had gotten her feet wet in politics —and she *had* been on the winning team.

CHAPTER 6

"She Can Lead"

The year 1960 was significant for black people in the United States of America. Down South the sit-ins had begun. Started by black college students, the new civil rights movement spread like fire until it reached the North. Even in Brooklyn, a new courage and militance were noticeable.

In 1960 a bright and personable black lawyer named Thomas R. Jones from the Bedford-Stuyvesant Political League gathered together a group of friends, both black and white, and founded the Unity Democratic Club. Jones declared as the club's candidate for state assemblyman.

Shirley was buzzing with news about the new club when Conrad came home from one of his trips. "This is something entirely new for the neighborhood," she said. "Jones feels that after all these years the Political League has the wrong approach to politics. He says we're never

67

going to get anywhere until we fight the machine politicians on their own ground—by forming a real Democratic club and challenging the old whites' only club for the party leadership in Bedford-Stuyvesant. Jones and his friends feel they can actually take over the party in this district."

"What does your friend Wesley Holder think?" Conrad asked.

Shirley made a face. "I don't think Wesley's going to go along with Jones," she said. "Those two just don't seem to like each other. But I think Wesley's wrong on this one. If we're ever going to get any real political power, we have to take control of the party machinery. The old club is strong because it gets patronage from the party. Half of the white club's captains have cushy jobs in City Hall—that's why they work so hard at campaign time."

"So after that analysis, Shirley, are you going to work in the Tom Jones campaign?" Conrad inquired.

"I do believe so," Shirley replied. "You know I'm an activist. I can't stay out of a good fight."

Shirley joined the Unity Club and soon became a vice-president. The small band of workers that Tom Jones had gathered fought hard that spring, but the odds were against them. Tom Jones lost to his white opponent in the Democratic primary.

"It isn't over yet," Shirley told Conrad. "Unity has made a name for itself in the neighborhood. We're going to conduct a big voter registration drive this fall."

"With the presidential race coming up in November, you ought to be able to register a lot of new voters."

"That's right," Shirley agreed thoughtfully. "The contest between John F. Kennedy and Richard Nixon will create a lot of voter interest. A lot of people who don't know anything about the local campaigns will want a chance to vote for the Preisdent. I told the club that my Spanish is good enough now for me to canvass the Puerto Rican people in this neighborhood. The Unity Club must stand for unity among black, white, and Puerto Rican."

"You're getting me so interested in this that I think I'm going to go down and join the Unity Club myself," Conrad decided.

"Wonderful!" his wife replied. "You'll be more than welcome."

Shirley's patient canvassing and the hard work of many others began to produce results. In 1962 the club was ready to try again.

Tom Jones was the club's candidate for State Assembly and for the party leader in the district. The Unity Club had attracted many new members by this time, and the executive committee had more than enough dedicated workers to appoint as club captains. Each club captain was in charge of a small election district—a few streets within the larger district from which Jones was running for the State Assembly. It was the job of each club captain to get out the vote in his election district on primary day. Shirley and Conrad were both assigned election districts, and they went out each night to talk to the voters on their lists.

When the votes were counted, Tom Jones had won the Democratic primary! In the general election two months later, Jones had no trouble at all beating his Republican opponent. The Unity Democratic Club was triumphant at last.

The New York State Legislature began its new term in January. Each Monday Tom Jones traveled to Albany, the state capital, to vote in the Assembly. When he returned to Brooklyn at the end of the week, he gave a progress report to the members of the Unity Club.*

Shirley was fascinated by Tom Jones's description of the political process in Albany. The more he talked, the more she wished that *she* could be the one who introduced bills and tried to steer them through their various stages all the way up to the governor.

"I'd better not start daydreaming," Shirley told her-

* See note 1, page 137

self firmly. "Tom Jones is our assemblyman and that's that. I have plenty of important work of my own to do."

Shirley had been appointed New York City's chief educational consultant for all of its day nurseries, and she spent her working days traveling from day care center to day care center, giving advice to the centers' directors and straightening out problems whenever they arose. She still found time, however, to be active in the Unity Club. In recognition of her organizing skills, the members had elected her coleader.

Assemblyman Jones was up for reelection in 1964, but an unusual thing happened. The leaders of Brooklyn's County Democratic organization came to him and asked him to be their candidate for civil court judge.

Jones called an urgent meeting of the Unity Club's executive committee to tell them about the surprise offer he had received. "I think I'm going to accept the nomination," Jones told the group. "It's a great honor to be asked to serve as a judge. What this means for the club is that we're going to have to find the best person we can to run for the Assembly—someone with real leadership ability. Go home and think it over and next week let's come back and discuss some names."

The members agreed and the meeting broke up. On her way to the door, Shirley overheard a few of the women talking among themselves.

"Why not give it to Shirley Chisholm?" one of them said loudly. "She can *lead!*"

"Why not give it to Chisholm?" another lady echoed. And another, "Why not?"

That night Shirley had a long talk with Conrad.

"With your energy and your ability to get things done, you'd do a wonderful job in the Assembly," her husband told her. "I think you ought to tell the executive board at the next meeting that you're interested in running."

"They'll never give it to me," Shirley said with a shake of her head. "No black woman has ever held an elective office in Brooklyn."

"You could be the first."

Shirley laughed. "That's what a professor of mine at Brooklyn College once told me. He always said I should go into politics."

"You've *been* in politics, Shirley, for many years. But now is the time for you to run for office. Don't you want to run for the Assembly?"

"Yes, I do," Shirley replied. "And I feel strong enough to win. But you do understand that this will change our life drastically. I'll have to quit my consultant's job with the city and I'll be away from home three or four days a week whenever the Legislature is in session."

"You always put up with my traveling, so I guess I can put up with yours," Conrad said gently.

1. "This is Fighting Shirley Chisholm" is the way the candidate began her street corner meetings. Here she demonstrates her campaign style while the television cameras grind away. "I love to campaign," Mrs. Chisholm says. *(Wide World Photos)*

2. Assemblywoman Chisholm addresses the New York State Legislature — Mrs. Chisholm spent four years in Albany representing her Bedford-Stuyvesant community in the State Legislature. She left to run for Congress after establishing a reputation for always doing her homework and never being afraid to jump into a debate. *(United Press International Photo)*

3. Famous victory photo of Shirley Chisholm, taken the night she won election to Congress. Mrs. Chisholm fooled the experts and beat her Republican opponent James Farmer by 2½ to 1. (*Wide World Photos*)

4. Husband Conrad pins an orchid on his victorious wife. Photo was taken in Washington on the day Shirley was sworn into office. "I never could have done it without Conrad," the congresswoman says. (*United Press International Photo*)

5. Outgoing President Lyndon Baines Johnson greets incoming Congresswoman Shirley Chisholm during her first week in Washington. As a child, Shirley wondered if her picture would ever be taken with a United States President. (*United Press International Photo*)

6. Nation's first black woman congressman is sworn into office by John McCormack, the Speaker of the House of Representatives. Mrs. Chisholm and McCormack later had a difference of opinion over her House Committee assignment, but they remain friends. (*Wide World Photos*)

7. On the steps of the Capitol, Congresswoman Shirley Chisholm
pauses for a moment's reflection. She carries with her the material she
plans to use in a speech before her House colleagues. "She socks it to
them," one newspaper said of her. (*Wide World Photos*)

8. Congresswoman Chisholm waits to testify at a congressional hearing with two fellow Democrats—John Conyers and Charles C. Diggs, Jr. Both men are congressmen from the state of Michigan. (*Wide World Photos*)

9. Congresswoman Chisholm addresses a news conference. She is flanked by three other Democratic congressmen from New York — Allard K. Lowenstein, Edward I. Koch, and William Fitts Ryan. (*United Press International Photo*)

10. Representative Chisholm meets with group that came to Washington to protest cuts in the poverty program. Mrs. Chisholm speaks out tirelessly for a massive man-power training program and for more aid to education. Her heavy speaking schedule around the nation when Congress is not in session keeps her continually on the go. *(United Press International Photo)*

11. Congresswoman Chisholm shares a laugh with Robert Finch, President Nixon's Secretary for Health, Education, and Welfare. Finch is a Republican, but he seeks out Mrs. Chisholm's views on education. Part of the Democratic congresswoman's job in Washington is getting along with the Republican Administration. *(United Press International Photo)*

12. Representative Chisholm breaks party ranks and endorses John Lindsay, a Liberal, for Mayor of New York City. The fearless Mrs. Chisholm campaigned actively for Lindsay, who won re-election. *(United Press International Photo)*

13. Like most other members of Congress from New York, Shirley Chisholm returns to her district on weekends. Here she meets with constituents in her Brooklyn office. *(Friedman-Abels)*

14. Congresswoman Chisholm talks to voters in her 12th Congressional District. "I never forget that it is the people who elected me," he says. *(Wide World Photos)* *(Ebony magazine)*

15. During a visit to a housing project in her Congressional District, Mrs. Chisholm stops to chat with some neighborhood children who easily recognized her. "I know you — you're Shirley Chisholm, you're my congressman," one of them said. *(Ebony magazine)*

16. Mrs. Chisholm pauses to chat with her husband Conrad during a stroll through her district. "She needs someone to watch out for the details, to look out for her, and see to it that she eats and sleeps properly," Conrad says. *(Ebony magazine)*

"As an assemblywoman I'd be a public figure," Shirley went on. "There would be meetings and dinners and speeches every night—I know what it would be like."

Conrad laughed. "Sounds like the life you're already leading. Only for the first time you'll actually get paid for being a politician."

"You really are in favor of it?" Shirley asked anxiously.

"I certainly am—because I know it's what you've wanted for a long time. Early in our marriage I knew you'd be the star in the family."

"I'm going to do it, Conrad," Shirley said suddenly. "I'm going in there at the next executive board meeting and tell them I'm ready to fight. I have my supporters, I know, and the rest will just have to be persuaded. Some of them won't like the idea of a woman running at all. I'll go in and say, 'Gentlemen, have your discussion if you need to have it. I want the nomination and I intend to fight for it. I'm the strongest candidate you have and I know I can win.' That ought to convince them I'm serious, don't you think?"

"I think the club will choose you, Shirley. In fact, I'm certain of it. Now let's get some sleep, Assemblywoman Chisholm."

The Unity Club *did* choose Shirley Chisholm as their candidate for the State Assembly. She went on to win the Democratic primary easily and the general election as well. In 1964 Mrs. Chisholm became the first black woman to be elected to public office in Brooklyn. She was forty years old.

CHAPTER 7

Assemblywoman Chisholm

"It's just my luck," Shirley said to Conrad, "that as soon as I get elected to the Assembly they start to change the district's lines."

Shirley was first elected to the State Assembly in 1964. The regular term for a New York State legislator is two years, but because the Legislature had decided to redraw the boundaries of some of its districts—in order to make the population distribution more even—Shirley had to run again in 1965 and 1966.

"Each time you run you get more votes," Conrad reminded his wife. "That means you're building up quite a reputation in Bedford-Stuyvesant."

"That's true," Shirley acknowledged. "My name is right at the bottom of the voting machine, but I always pull higher than the top of the ticket. I can't walk down the street now without some people recognizing me. They expect me to do a job for them in Albany."

"And you must be doing what they want or they wouldn't keep voting you back into office."

By now Shirley was an experienced legislator. Even the traveling to and from Albany, which she had found very tiresome in the beginning, was by now second nature. She had gotten used to the pace.

Every Monday, along with the other legislators from New York City, she made the trip up to the state's capital by train or bus. The legislature met from January to April, and the closer it got to April the more the work load increased. At the start of the session in January, Shirley was often back in Brooklyn by Tuesday night or Wednesday. But by the time March rolled around, the Assembly met every week until Friday afternoon.

Sometimes the Assembly carried on its debates into the evening. When the day's—or evening's—work was over, Shirley packed up a load of bills she wanted to study and went back to her hotel room. The Dewitt Clinton Hotel was right across the street from the Capitol Building, and most of the legislators stayed there.

"I hate to think of you spending every night cooped up in that small hotel room," Conrad said to his wife.

"I don't mind it so much," Shirley replied. "I order my dinner served in my room and I've got the TV. And besides, it's a good place to do my legislative homework.

They don't give us much office space in that State Capitol Building."

"Don't the other legislators ever ask you to go out to dinner with them?" Conrad asked. "I can't believe *they're* spending all their evenings in the hotel."

Shirley laughed. "I think some of them are a little afraid of me. Most men don't like independent women, you know that. The first time I got up to speak in the Assembly I could feel their eyes on me. They're not used to a strong woman who isn't afraid to speak her mind. They're not like you, Conrad. They don't know I'm a regular gal."

Since her freshman year in the legislature, Shirley had never been afraid to jump into a debate. After all, a champion debater from Brooklyn College was trained to speak forcefully on her own feet, and the years she had spent participating in the Unity Club's meetings had also given her confidence in the State Assembly.

The Assembly chamber was large and impressive. Shirley and the other legislators sat in rows of green leather chairs with long polished wooden desks in front of them. The Republicans sat on one side of the aisle and the Democrats on the other.

When Shirley wished to talk on a particular bill before the Assembly, she had to wait until she was recognized by the Speaker. The Speaker is the most powerful man in the Assembly. He sits on a raised stage in front of the chamber and directs debates and keeps order by loud raps of his wooden gavel.

Shirley discovered there were many bills that came before the Assembly that she wanted to speak about.

"Those legislators who represent the rural communities in upstate New York just don't have any idea what life is like in a big city ghetto," she told Conrad. "I have to really be a voice of Bedford-Stuyvesant in Albany. I have to explain to them some of the horrible facts of poverty—the overcrowded tenements, the rats and roaches, and the lack of jobs and the great need for training programs so the jobless can learn new skills."

"Do they listen to you?" Conrad inquired.

"I think they do," Shirley replied. "At least they get awfully quiet when I take the microphone to speak. I think I've been able to change some minds on some of the bills."

Shirley Chisholm had nine bills of her own passed by the Assembly during the four years that she served in Albany. Four of them were signed into law.

Her first proud accomplishment was a bill to extend unemployment insurance coverage to domestic workers.

"This will be the first time in the history of New York State that maids and cleaning women will be covered by the unemployment insurance laws," Shirley told the Assembly. "My own mother worked as a domestic for forty cents an hour when my sisters and I were growing up. She scrubbed floors on her hands and knees in other people's homes so she could keep our family together. But when there was no more work for my mother—when the people she worked for moved, or decided to go on vacation—suddenly my mother was without a source of income, *through no fault of her own.*

"When a worker in a factory or an office is let go because there is no more work for him to do, he is entitled to unemployment insurance—a weekly amount of money to keep him going until he is able to find another job. This bill of mine will extend the same benefits to domestic workers."

The Chisholm bill to extend unemployment insurance to domestic workers passed the Assembly easily. A similar bill was also passed in the Senate, and then New York's Governor Nelson A. Rockefeller signed it into law.

The Democratic leaders in the Assembly decided that because of Shirley's teaching background, it made good sense to assign her to the Committee on Education.

"I'm really pleased with this assignment," Shirley reported back to the Unity Club. "Not every legislator gets a committee assignment that he's interested in.

With my knowledge of the public school system and my professional work with the city's day care centers I ought to be able to make some important contributions to the education laws of this state."

Every assemblyman and state senator in Albany is pursued by the men and women known as lobbyists.* Shirley discovered some of the lobbyists who represented powerful organizations and industries seemed to have a lot of money to spend. They were always giving lavish cocktail parties and dinners for the legislators at the Dewitt Clinton or one of the other Albany hotels.

Shirley very seldom went to a dinner that was given by one of the lobbyists. "I don't like the idea at all," she said to Conrad. "It's almost as if they're trying to buy my vote. You know—they do you a favor and then you're supposed to do them a favor. Some of the better legislators feel the same way I do about it. We check with each other whenever we get an invitation to see who else is going."

"Some of those lobbyists probably hand out a lot more than a free dinner," Conrad said with a laugh.

"I think you're absolutely right," Shirley replied. "Sometimes after a certain vote I hear rumors about how so-and-so was given such-and-such for his vote. It's better

* See note 2, pages 137–38

to stay away from personal contact with lobbyists—unless of course they're from an organization that I know and approve of, like the NAACP."

One person who was doing lobbying work in Albany and whom Shirley did get friendly with was named Julius C. C. Edelstein. He was a professor with the City University of New York and he was in Albany for a very special project.

Professor Edelstein was in Albany to get support for a new educational program known as SEEK. The initials stood for "Search for Education, Elevation, and Knowledge." SEEK was a plan to give state scholarships to bright black and Puerto Rican kids whose parents did not have the money to give their children a college education.

What made SEEK special was that its sponsors recognized that the education these young men and women received in their ghetto public schools and high schools was poor. So, along with the scholarship money went a program of additional education and counseling so that the scholarship students could keep up with the regular college work.

The SEEK program needed a large sum of money from the legislature in order to get off the ground. Professor Edelstein sought out Shirley Chisholm and asked her to do what she could for the bill in her Education committee.

Shirley took an instant liking to the gray-haired professor, and she thought the SEEK program was an important piece of legislation. She made the passage of the bill her own special project.

In the Education committee and on the floor of the Assembly, Shirley talked long and hard about the need for special scholarships for Negro and Puerto Rican youths, to give them the same opportunities that more privileged white youths received. She spoke from her own experience about what education had done for her, and she spoke of others less fortunate than she who were trapped in dead-end jobs for life because they could not get a higher education.

"It makes me sick and angry to think of the hundreds of thousands of brains that have been lost to America because they never had the opportunity to go to college," she told the Assembly. "The SEEK bill will give funds to Negro and Puerto Rican youths who show that they have the potential. A lot of these young people come from ghetto schools with poor curriculums and teachers who think that their students must be inferior because they are black. They graduate with dead-end vocational diplomas. They are not able to compete with white children for college scholarships. These children are the victims of discrimination and segregation. We *must* show them that there is hope for them in this land."

Shirley's words moved her fellow assemblymen. The SEEK program got its money. In the first two years of operation, eight thousand young people were granted SEEK scholarships to New York State colleges.

CHAPTER 8

A Black Woman in Congress?

In 1968, the New York State Legislature set up a committee to redraw some of the congressional district lines in central Brooklyn.* While they were at it, the big political leaders decided that since the black population of Brooklyn was quite large—and all the congressmen from Brooklyn were white—it made sense to redraw the lines in such a way that one new congressional district in Brooklyn was built around the black neighborhood of Bedford-Stuyvesant. That way it was assured that in the next election Brooklyn would be sending a black representative to Congress for the first time in history.

The new congressional district was to be known as the 12th CD. Even before the boundaries of the "new 12th" were made public, the neighborhood of Bedford-Stuyvesant was buzzing with the news. A black representative in Congress from Bedford-Stuyvesant! The only other

* See note 3, pages 138–39

black man in Congress from the state of New York was Adam Clayton Powell who represented Harlem. Now he would be joined by someone from Brooklyn. Who would the new representative be?

The newspapers ran several stories filled with names and speculation. A certain well-known minister was picking up support; a certain civil rights leader was said to be interested. On and on the speculation went. Whom would the Democrats choose as their candidate? Would the party leaders get together and select one candidate or would there be a primary fight? Whom would the Republicans choose? What would the Liberal Party do?

One cold evening in February, when Shirley returned to Brooklyn from her week's work in Albany, she heard the front doorbell ring.

"Are we expecting anybody?" she asked Conrad as she went to the door.

Standing on the front stoop was an elderly Negro woman. "Mrs. Chisholm," the lady said, "my friends and I know what you've been doing for us up there in Albany. We want *you* to run for Congress from this neighborhood. We collected this money and we want to give it to you for a campaign contribution."

Shirley was flabbergasted. She ushered the woman inside the house.

"It isn't much," said the woman as she offered Shirley

an envelope. "We don't have much to give. But it's a beginning and we're going to go out and collect more."

Inside the envelope Shirley found $9.62—all in coins. With tears streaming down her face, she hugged the lady tightly. "I know what this money means to you," she whispered. "We'll make it together—you and I."

Later that night, after the woman had left, Shirley carefully wrapped the envelope of coins in a handkerchief and put it away in the top drawer of her dresser.

"I'm going to keep this envelope intact always," she said to Conrad. "That woman has probably spent her whole life working as a domestic. She could have been my own mother. Women like that are worth more to me than the opinions of a thousand politicians."

"I've been wondering when you were going to start thinking about that congressional seat," Conrad replied.

"Oh, I've been thinking about it all right," Shirley said. "The black legislators in Albany have been talking about nothing else for months."

"Your Assembly District is the heart of the new Congressional District," Conrad said with a smile as he lit his pipe. "It seems to me that you'd be the logical choice of the party leaders."

"Never," Shirley replied. "I'm too independent for them. I'd never be the choice of the Brooklyn County organization. I've walked out of meetings of party leaders

87

here and in Albany when I haven't liked the position they were taking. I've never been in favor with the bigwigs in the Brooklyn organization. They'll want someone for that congressional seat that they think they can control."

"The Unity Club is behind you one hundred per cent, we know that," Conrad said thoughtfully. "I wonder what the other clubs in the district will be doing."

"I saw a map of the new 12th in Albany last week," Shirley reported. "The district goes clear up to the Queens line. It takes in parts of Williamsburg, Crown Heights, and Bushwick. Those districts are controlled by white leaders. I expect that the white leaders won't try to field a candidate of their own, but you can be sure that they'll all get together behind one of the black candidates—and it won't be me."

"I've never known you to be so pessimistic."

"I'm just being realistic," reported Shirley. "The white male leaders will feel more comfortable dealing with a black man than with a black woman. It's as simple as that. Besides, they'll think they're being super-liberal by supporting a male candidate. All that talk about the need to strengthen the image of black men is going to make them try to stop Shirley Chisholm, you mark my words. That will be their solution to the problems of Bedford-Stuyvesant: put a man in the office—as if we black women have ever held important political jobs!"

"Well, the women of Bedford-Stuyvesant might feel as angry about this male business as you do," Conrad said to his wife. "The women have always supported your candidacy. If the lady who came to the door tonight is any indication, they *want* you to run."

A few evenings later Conrad came home to find his wife poring over a set of large books.

"I see you wasted no time in getting hold of the election rolls,"* he said to Shirley with a grin. "Before you tell me anything, I've got something to tell you. I was walking down Fulton Street today and I saw a JONES FOR CONGRESS store front that had just opened up. Your old friend Judge Tom Jones apparently would like to run for Congress too."

Shirley raised her eyebrows. "I heard that Tom was interested," she replied. "And I heard he has a powerful friend in his corner."

"What do you mean?"

"From what I understand, Senator Robert Kennedy and Jones are very close," Shirley said with a sigh. "If Kennedy comes into this district to campaign for Tom, it might swing a lot of votes."

"I don't think Kennedy would interfere with a local

* See note 4, page 139

race," Conrad said slowly. "That's not good politics. Besides, your name carries as much weight in Bedford-Stuyvesant as Kennedy's does. The people here *know* you and know what you've done for them."

"It really hurts me," Shirley went on, "that in all the years I've been in politics here, Robert Kennedy never sought me out."

"Maybe there were some people who kept him from you," Conrad offered. "You know how politicians are. If he'd have asked me, I'd have told him the person to see in Bedford-Stuyvesant is named Shirley Chisholm."

"Well, I guess I shouldn't brood about it," Shirley said with a shrug.

Conrad changed the subject. "What have you learned so far from studying the election rolls?"

Shirley lit up instantly. "It's fascinating, Conrad. You can tell so much about a neighborhood from just looking at the names of the registered voters. Bedford-Stuyvesant is mostly all black, we know that already. The 12th CD seems to have a lot of Italians in the Bushwick section and a lot of Jews in Crown Heights. And I'm amazed at how many Puerto Rican names show up on the election rolls in Williamsburg."

"You've always gotten along well with all kinds of people," Conrad said as he leafed through the pages. "And you'll probably be the only candidate who can speak Spanish fluently. You'll do very well with the Puerto Rican vote."

"That's what I'm counting on," Shirley agreed. "There's something else here, Conrad, that is very interesting. I want to examine it more closely."

"What did you discover?"

"I haven't done any arithmetic yet, so I don't have the exact figures, but it appears that there are thousands more women voters in this district than men."

"That *is* interesting," Conrad agreed. "The women voters have always been fierce about you, Shirley. The 12th CD is looking better all the time."

Shirley Chisholm announced her candidacy for Congress the following week. Shortly afterward, a fellow legislator from Bedford-Stuyvesant, State Senator William C. Thompson, declared he was also in the race. Neither announcement got any attention in the city's newspapers or on television.

A few weeks later, when the Chisholms were eating a quiet dinner at home, a friend from the Unity Club telephoned.

"Quick, Shirley, turn on the TV to the evening news," the friend said hurriedly.

Shirley switched on the television set. She and Conrad watched as James Farmer, the former national director of CORE—the Congress of Racial Equality—declared his candidacy for Congress from Brooklyn's 12th District.

Shirley and Conrad looked unbelievingly at the television screen.

"But he doesn't even *live* in Brooklyn," Shirley sputtered. "He lives in Manhattan."

"They're certainly giving him a big play on the evening news," Conrad remarked.

The Chisholms listened as Farmer gave his reasons for entering the race.

"So he says the rats and roaches don't stop at the Brooklyn Bridge," Shirley said bitterly. "Well, why doesn't he do something about the rats in Harlem? Why is he so interested in Bedford-Stuyvesant all of a sudden?"

"Calm down," Conrad said to his wife. "He's only got the Liberal Party nomination. The Liberals don't carry much weight in Bedford-Stuyvesant."

"He's starting out with the Liberal nomination," Shirley replied. "Maybe he'll pick up the Republican nomination as well. Or maybe he thinks we'll all fold up and he'll get the Democratic nomination too."

"Don't you think the local Republicans will want to name their own candidate?" Conrad asked.

"You heard the television commentator call him a

national figure. Farmer's entry into the race might change the whole picture."

"What are you going to do about it?"

"I'm going to call a campaign meeting for tomorrow night. I'd better get right on the telephone. So it's not only going to be a tough primary fight—it's going to be a battle right up until November. Where's my telephone book? I've got to tell some people that the time has come —we've got to go to war!"

CHAPTER 9

"This Is Fighting Shirley Chisholm"

"The first order of business is putting together a good campaign committee," Shirley said proudly to Conrad. "And I've certainly done that. I deserve to win just because the people who are supporting me are so good."

Shirley had asked her old friend Wesley Holder to be her campaign manager, and Holder, now in his early seventies, had plotted the campaign strategy.

Everyone agreed that Shirley's base of strength was her own 55th Assembly District. That was the district she represented in Albany, and everybody in the neighborhood knew her. The Unity Democratic Club was solidly behind her, and the district leader, Thomas R. Fortune, could be counted on to turn out a large vote for Shirley Chisholm.

"First things first," Holder had said to Shirley. "Our first job is to win the Democratic primary. If you take the primary against the other Democratic candidates, you'll have no trouble at all winning the general election. This district has always been heavily Democratic, so the winner of the primary should sail through the general election in November. That means that Tommy Fortune has to get out every available vote in the 55th."

"Don't worry about the 55th," Fortune had assured them. "Everybody in the club and the neighborhood is behind Shirley. We'll be out ringing doorbells every night of the week till primary day. Shirley will carry this part of her new Congressional District by better than three to one."

Shirley smiled happily. She knew she could count on Tommy Fortune and her friends in Unity.

"What about the other sections of the new 12th CD where they don't know me personally?" she asked Holder. "Have you figured out a battle plan?"

"You're going to get an organization of your women supporters together," Holder said enthusiastically. "The women will fan out over the entire district with shopping bags full of campaign leaflets. You, Shirley, will be out on a sound truck a good deal of the time—acquainting the voters with your personality and your stand on the issues."

"I guess we'll be wanting bumper stickers too," Conrad put in. "Signs that say CHISHOLM FOR CONGRESS that people can stick on their car bumpers. The bumper stickers and the leaflets and the sound truck will take a lot of money, though, won't they?"

"Most of the money will be raised from people in the 12th Congressional District who want to see Shirley Chisholm in Congress," Holder said thoughtfully. "But it would be helpful if Shirley can scare up some extra money from some of her city-wide contacts. I don't expect that we're going to get any money from this primary fight from the Brooklyn Democratic County organization."

"Not likely," Shirley laughed. "Since the organization is not supporting my candidacy. I think I know someone, Wesley, who might do some fund-raising for me. His name is Julius Edelstein and we worked together very closely in Albany to push through the SEEK program."

"He sounds like a good bet," Holder said with a nod. "Now, the next item on our agenda is to settle on a good campaign slogan—one that sums up in a few words what your candidacy is all about. Got any ideas, Shirley?"

Shirley thought for a minute before she spoke. "Well, since the big party leaders aren't supporting me—because they know they can't control my votes—and since everyone who knows me knows I always speak my own mind, how about UNBOUGHT AND UNBOSSED for a campaign slogan?"

Wesley Holder nodded vigorously. "UNBOUGHT AND UNBOSSED suits you to a T, Shirley. That's what it'll be."

Shirley's opponents in the Democratic primary were State Senator William C. Thompson and Dollie Robinson, a former state labor department official. Thomas R. Jones had dropped out of the race to run instead for a State Supreme Court judgeship.

Shirley's campaign organization got under way. The day of the primary was set for June 18.

Speaking to voters from the top of a sound truck was nothing new to Shirley Chisholm. Her races for the State Assembly had given her plenty of experience with campaigns.

"I really like to campaign," Shirley told Conrad one weekend evening when she had spent the entire day making short street corner speeches to voters in the new 12th Congressional District. "The people really listen to what I have to say. It's important to get close to the voters—to let them see you and to shake their hands."

Shirley and Conrad and some members of the Chisholm campaign staff rode the sound truck from stop to stop. Other members of the candidate's team rode behind them in private cars. The Chisholm campaign caravan looked impressive. "The people have to know that I have a good organization of supporters behind me," Shirley told her campaign workers.

98

The street corner meetings were tough and exhausting. Sometimes while Shirley was at the microphone, a heckler would walk by and interrupt her speech with a catcall. Shirley had to have a smart answer ready for him or else there might be jeers and laughter and the meeting would get out of hand.

Shirley's favorite campaign stops were at the public housing projects. Her campaign caravan would drive right into one of the streets of the big projects and Shirley would take the microphone.

"Ladies and gentlemen of the Brevoort Houses, this is Fighting Shirley Chisholm coming through," she would announce in a firm, strong voice.

Her opening statement over the loudspeaker and the sight of campaign cars covered with Chisholm stickers were usually enough to draw a crowd at the projects.

While Shirley was talking to the residents of the housing project, and reminding them to come out and vote for her on primary day, her campaign workers would scatter through the crowd with their shopping bags full of campaign leaflets.

By the time Shirley had finished her speech, the crowd had always tripled in size, and her campaign staff had handed out something like two thousand leaflets. Then Shirley would climb down from the sound truck and begin to shake hands. She knew so many of the voters who lived in the projects that she always got a warm welcome from them. They in turn were always pleased that a candidate for Congress had taken the trouble to visit with them right where they lived.

"Judging from the response at the projects, I don't think I'm doing too badly in this campaign," Shirley said to Conrad after a particularly successful afternoon at the projects.

Shirley didn't like to admit that she was worried. Her long-time ally Tommy Fortune had told her that most of the other political leaders in the new 12th Congressional District considered State Senator Thompson to be an easy winner.

"They're even willing to bet money," Fortune had laughed.

"What do you think?" Shirley had asked the Unity Club's leader.

"I think you'll make it," Fortune had answered. "In fact, I think I'm going to take some of those bets. I'd like to win a little money on primary day."

The third black candidate in the race, Dollie Robinson, didn't bother Shirley. "Some people think that Dollie's going to cut into my vote because she's a woman," she told Conrad. "But I don't think so. Dollie's from the same part of the district as Willie Thompson, and I think they're going to hurt each other, and not me."

There *was* a serious complication to the primary race, however, and Shirley was well aware of it. That spring the nation's eyes were on the presidential primaries. In the Democratic party, the fighting was particularly bitter.

Shirley watched the contest for the Democratic presidential nomination with keen interest. First there was Senator Eugene McCarthy of Minnesota, who surprised everybody by almost beating President Lyndon Johnson in New Hampshire. Then Senator Robert Kennedy of New York announced that he was also going to challenge President Johnson. After that, President Johnson startled the nation by declaring that he was not going to run for President again at all, and soon Vice-President Hubert Humphrey announced that he was now a candidate for President.

"The war in Vietnam is really pulling the Democratic party apart," Shirley said sorrowfully to Conrad. "I wouldn't be surprised if it costs us the presidential election in November."

Over the last years Shirley had begun to question the Vietnam War. "I don't understand a country that spends billions of dollars to fight a war thousands of miles from our shores when right here at home there isn't enough money to fight sickness, hunger, and unemployment," she often told the voters from the sound truck.

As strongly as Shirley felt about the war and other national issues, she didn't think that it was good politics for her to identify herself publicly with any of the candidates who were trying for the Democratic presidential nomination.

"I want the people in this district to choose one of the three of us for Congress on the basis of who *we* are, not on whom we're supporting for President," she used to say at meetings.

Two weeks before the New York primary, tragedy struck in California. Robert Kennedy was shot down by an assassin's bullet.

Kennedy's assassination had come two months after the assassination of Dr. Martin Luther King. It was a bad time for the country. No one in New York or in the rest of the nation could think about campaigns and politics.

The city was still numb from the shock of Kennedy's assassination when primary day, June 18, rolled around. All day long Shirley's supporters worked to get out the vote in the 12th Congressional District. By the time the polls closed in the evening, slightly more than twelve thousand registered Democrats had gone into the voting booths. The turnout had been small, there was no denying it, but the important question was: which candidate had gotten the most votes?

The counting of the votes went quickly. Each small election district had a modern voting machine, and when the back of the machine was opened up by the election inspectors, the number of votes Shirley and each of the others had received was clearly marked on the automatic counters. The election inspectors carefully marked down the numbers on their official forms and the forms were taken down to the Board of Elections with a police escort.

Unless the vote is very close, politicians never wait for the official results to be announced by the Board of Elections. They want to know immediately who has won so they station "poll watchers" at each polling place. The poll watchers copy down the figures from each voting machine at the same time the official election inspectors record the figures—and then the poll watchers run back to the candidates' headquarters with the precious information.

At Shirley's campaign headquarters, Wesley Holder sat at a desk with long sheets of paper in front of him. As the poll watchers brought in the results from each small election district—each precinct—in the 12th Congressional District, he entered the figures in three columns, labeled Chisholm, Thompson, and Robinson.

The all-important figures for Shirley's old Assembly District came in first. Holder turned to Shirley with a big smile.

"You're carrying the 55th by better than three to one," he told the candidate. "The Unity Club really did its job well."

Shirley looked over the figures and nodded. She was too nervous to speak. There were fifty-four small election districts in the 55th Assembly District and she had done beautifully in all of them. Now the important question was whether she would hold her own in the rest of the Congressional District, where she wasn't as well known.

Shirley's headquarters was turning into a madhouse as more and more campaign workers came in to report results from the outlying districts. The smell of victory was in the air.

Finally Holder stood up and chalked the totals on a big blackboard:

CHISHOLM	5680
THOMPSON	4907
ROBINSON	1848

A roar went up from Shirley's campaign workers. Shirley Chisholm had won the Democratic nomination for Congress!

The victorious candidate had won half her battle. The general election in November remained to be won.

When Shirley and Conrad went home late that night, they had a very serious matter to discuss between them. Shirley's health had gotten run down during the hard months of campaigning, and she and Conrad knew that she would have to enter the hospital for an operation. Shirley had postponed it as long as she could.

Shirley entered the hospital in July. She was back on her feet, but frail and weak, in August.

The National Democratic Convention was held in Chicago at the end of August. Shirley decided not to attend because she felt the trip would be too strenuous for her health. But something happened to make her change her mind. Tommy Fortune called from Chicago to say that the Democrats wanted to elect her as National Committeewoman from the state of New York, an important party office.

Still weak, Shirley was bundled onto a plane and flown to Chicago for the honor. The Democrats' convention turned out to be a violent event as the Chicago police battled war protesters in the streets. Shirley never ventured outside of her hotel room. She watched the battles in the streets and the politicking inside the convention hall on a television set in her room.

When New York's delegation elected her National

Committeewoman, she got the news from Tommy Fortune on the telephone. On the last day of the convention, the Democrats nominated Hubert Humphrey and Edmund Muskie as their candidates for President and Vice-President.

The violence in Chicago had left a bad taste in everyone's mouth. As Shirley flew back to New York, she couldn't help but wonder how much the events in Chicago would hurt the Democratic candidates against the Republicans Richard Nixon and Spiro Agnew.

Back in Brooklyn, Shirley's campaign organization began preparing for "Stage Two"—the general election in November. Shirley's major opponent was James Farmer, who had gotten the Republican nomination as well as the Liberal Party nomination. The Conservative Party had put up a white man named Ralph J. Carrano, but nobody gave him much of a chance.

Campaign manager Holder gave Shirley his thinking on the kind of campaign they needed to wage:

"Farmer's strategy is going to be that you're a gracious lady with the right ideas, but that the 12th Congressional District needs a man for the job," he told her. "He's going to appeal to the top of the pyramid—to the intellectuals who have followed his career in the newspapers. Now, Shirley, don't waste your time trying to reach those voters—there aren't that many of them. You concentrate on the broad base of the pyramid that has all the average voters who know you as a local figure."

Shirley nodded in agreement. "I checked the election rolls long before I got into this race," she said to Holder. "And my research turned up the fact that there are about twelve thousand more women voters registered in this district than men. Farmer's strategy might just backfire on him at that."

Shirley was still recovering from her operation so she could do little of the rugged street campaigning that she had done for the primary. The few speeches that she did give were at indoor meetings at some political and social clubs and at churches and synagogues in the neighborhood. Now that she was the regular Democratic candidate for Congress, Brooklyn's County Democratic organization, which had ignored her in the primary, came forward to help her by arranging meetings in the white parts of the district.

Her opponent's campaign, by contrast, was loud and noisy. Farmer's campaign managers used bongo players to drum up a crowd for the candidate's street meetings. The young men who handed out his leaflets often wore *dashikis*—the African-style shirt that was becoming popular among the young militants. As Wesley Holder had predicted, Farmer's speeches and his leaflets stressed the need for "a man's voice" in Washington.

One of Shirley's close supporters came to her one day and said, "You'd better get back on the streets with your sound truck, Mrs. Chisholm. That Farmer is making hay out there with the voters."

Shirley shook her head. Whenever she and Farmer met face to face for a debate, her positions were just as militant as his were, and the people who listened knew that she could do more than hold her own with him—despite her being a "mere woman." Besides that fact, there were three other reasons why she felt confident that she would win in November by continuing with her quiet kind of campaigning:

First, she had her women—and men—supporters who in Conrad's words were "fierce" about her.

Second, she knew from talking to people in the neighborhood that many voters resented the fact that Farmer, who lived in Manhattan, had come into Brooklyn to run for Congress. "It's saying to the people here that you have nobody worthwhile for this $30,000 fruitcake," she often said in her speeches. (The annual salary for a congressman was then $30,000.)

Third, Shirley knew that Central Brooklyn had always voted heavily Democratic, and *she* was the regular Democratic candidate.

With these factors going for her, how could she lose? In Shirley's logical mind it was all very simple, but to her constant annoyance, the city's newspapers and television news programs continued to ignore her while they played up her opponent's candidacy.

"The only newspaper that seems to know I'm alive is *The Amsterdam News*," she said irritably to Conrad one day.

One weekend they watched a national television news special about the campaign in Brooklyn's 12th Congressional District. The half-hour network program was mostly devoted to James Farmer. There were only a few scenes of Shirley's campaign.

After the show, some of Shirley's supporters called the television station to complain. They were told that since Shirley's opponent was a "national figure" and since his campaign was "so colorful" the program had concentrated on him.

Shirley burned, but there was nothing she could do about it.

"After you win in November, *you're* going to be a national figure, Shirley," her husband said to console her.

Election Day—November 5, 1968—finally arrived. Shirley's campaign organization worked smoothly to turn out the vote. By this time they were experienced hands at getting voters to the polls.

The lines at the polling places were long and the voters

often had to wait for more than an hour before they could go in and cast their votes.

In Shirley's own election district, she had the opportunity to vote for several familiar names. Thomas R. Jones was on the ballot for State Supreme Court judge and Thomas R. Fortune was on the ballot for assemblyman. And there, in a prominent spot on the machine, was the name Shirley Chisholm for congressman!

Shirley and Conrad voted early in the morning. Then Shirley toured the other polling places in her district with some of her campaign workers, to say hello to the election inspectors and poll watchers she knew.

"It's been a long campaign," Shirley said to Conrad at dinner. "It's been nine months since I first announced for Congress, and six months since I started to campaign actively for the nomination. Well, I've done everything I could do to convince the voters that I'm the right choice. If the people don't want me I guess I can always go back to being a professional educator."

The polls stayed open till ten o'clock that night. Early in the evening Shirley went to her campaign headquarters and climbed a flight of stairs that led to a small, private room. Downstairs some of her supporters were fixing things up for a victory celebration, but Shirley was too nervous to see anybody. She preferred to stay upstairs with her husband and a few close friends until the election was decided.

Shortly before midnight there was no longer any doubt about the outcome of the race for Congress in Brooklyn's new 12th Congressional District. Shirley Chisholm was the winner! She had been overwhelmingly elected by the people in her district to represent them in the United States Congress in Washington!

The final figures were:

SHIRLEY CHISHOLM—Democrat	35239
JAMES FARMER—Republican	8929
—Liberal	4686
	13615
RALPH CARRANO—Conservative	4079

With tears in her eyes, Shirley walked downstairs to greet her campaign workers. A roar went up from the crowded hall as she made her entrance.

It was a proud moment in American history. Shirley Chisholm was the first black person to be elected to Congress from the borough of Brooklyn. Even more significant, Shirley Chisholm was the first black woman to be elected to Congress in the entire nation!

She had done it with the help of her close supporters,

but the victory was truly hers. She had worked for many years to reach her goal. The campaign headquarters was in a turmoil. Their own Shirley Chisholm had won. She was going to Congress!

The television and newspaper reporters who had ignored her for the past nine months were swarming around her for interviews. CBS, NBC, and ABC wanted to put her immediately on network television. The New York *Times*, the *Daily News*, the New York *Post*, the Associated Press and *The Amsterdam News* all wanted a statement. The photographers were busy snapping her victory photographs.

Shirley held up a "V for Victory" sign. When the husband, Conrad," she said quietly. "He stood by me crowd quieted down a little she began to speak.

"I never could have done it without the help of my one hundred per cent all the way. It is a great honor to be chosen as the nation's first black congresswoman. As a United States Representative in Washington, I intend to represent all the people—the blacks, the whites, the men, the women, and especially the youth. There are many new ideas abroad in this country, and I intend to speak for those ideas. And my voice will be heard."

CHAPTER 10

First Black Congresswoman

The telephone never stopped ringing at the Chisholm house from the moment Shirley's victory was announced.

Shirley and Conrad took turns answering it. Sometimes the caller was a dear, close friend who wanted to offer personal congratulations. But more often the caller was a newspaper, television, or radio reporter who wanted an exclusive interview about what it was like to be the first black woman ever elected to the United States Congress.

The reporters were not only from New York City. They called from across the nation. Shirley Chisholm had indeed become a national figure overnight.

Shirley tried to say no to some of the requests for interviews, but it was a losing battle. Reporters, she discovered, were very persistent when they wanted a story —and Shirley Chisholm was news. Reporters on newspapers in Israel, France, and Germany came to her house to see her. *Ebony* magazine did a cover story on her, and so did *The New York Times Magazine*. A British writer did a whole chapter on her life story for a book he was writing on the 1968 campaign. Even *Vogue* magazine asked her to come to their studios for a formal photograph. And then there were the young student reporters who represented their high school and college newspapers. Shirley found she could never say no to the student journalists.

After two weeks of nonstop interviews, Shirley's throat was sore from all the talking. She and Conrad flew to Jamaica to visit with Conrad's relatives—and hopefully to get some needed relaxation.

But even on the island of Jamaica Shirley was now an important celebrity. Reporters and well-wishers followed the Chisholms wherever they went walking in the city of Kingston. Shirley's picture had been in the papers, and everybody seemed to recognize her. They all wanted to kiss her or shake her hand.

Back in New York again, more interviews. While the Chisholms had been away, Wesley Holder had received more than five hundred letters and telegrams from newspapers, magazines, and radio and television stations that wanted special interviews. Each one, it seemed, had a different angle. The political reporters wanted a political interview. The women's page reporters wanted a special slant on Shirley Chisholm as a woman. The reporters from the national Negro press naturally wanted a story on the newest black representative in Congress.

Things were happening so fast that Shirley could hardly catch her breath. One of the last acts that the old session of Congress attended to was a salary raise for its members for the coming year. Shirley had thought that she had been elected to a $30,000 a year position, but the United States Congress upped the salary for representatives to $42,500.

"That's almost three times as much as I was making in Albany as a state assemblywoman," Shirley said proudly to Conrad. "Now we can pool our resources and buy that home of our own that we've been dreaming of."

Shirley and Conrad found a lovely nine-room attached row house on St. John's Place, just a few blocks from their old rented home. The people who sold the house to them also sold them a fine baby grand piano that occupied a place of honor in the living room.

Shirley had less than a month left before she would be officially inaugurated into office at the beginning of January. She and Conrad moved into the new house and she began the job of decorating the living room.

"The upstairs rooms are just going to have to wait,"

she said to her husband. "I don't know when I'm going to find the time to unpack the rest of these cartons."

The Chisholms went to Washington to find an apartment for Shirley to live in while Congress was in session.

"I think I'd better take something already furnished," Shirley said to Conrad. "My real home will always be in Brooklyn—in the 12th Congressional District." She found a furnished efficiency suite that looked nice enough and signed the lease. Shirley's next chore was to find a competent, experienced staff for her Washington congressional office.

"Since I won't know my way around the Capitol for the first month or so, I'd like to hire a staff that is already familiar with the workings of Congress," Shirley said to Congressman Joseph Resnick one day.

Resnick had an idea. He himself had not run for re-election. His own staff was excellent—and the girls were looking for jobs for the coming term.

Shirley interviewed Resnick's staff and decided to hire three of them. Travis Cain, a young black woman from Texas, would be her administrative assistant. Shirley Downs, a young white woman from upstate New York, would be her legislative assistant. Blond, friendly Karen McRorey, the third girl from Resnick's office, was hired to handle casework. The new congresswoman found the perfect personal secretary in Carolyn Jones, a sophisticated young black woman who came from the office of Representative Charles Whalen of Ohio.

"I think you must have the youngest, prettiest congressional staff in Washington," Conrad said, laughing, when he was introduced to the girls.

"They work well together as a team," Shirley answered. "And that's what's important."

Shirley was assigned to a convenient street floor suite in the Longworth Building. She and Conrad went to look it over. There was an outer office for her staff and a large private office for her.

The 435 United States Representatives were spread out in three separate office buildings—all connected to each other and to the House side of the Capitol Building by a system of tunnels, elevators, escalators, and passageways.

Shirley and Conrad did some exploring and promptly got lost in a maze of marble corridors.

"I wonder how long it will take before I can find my way around here?" Shirley said to Conrad as they walked over to a uniformed guard to ask for directions.

"The House Chamber is right this way, Mrs. Chisholm," the guard said cheerfully. "And congratulations on your splendid victory."

Shirley and her husband walked into the House of Representatives. The fine brown leather chairs and

117

polished wood desks looked a bit like the Assembly in Albany—but much more magnificent and perhaps three times the size.

Shirley's eyes scanned the Visitors' Gallery and then traveled across the rows of empty desks.

"Just think," she whispered to Conrad. "In one month *I'll* be sitting in one of those leather chairs."

CHAPTER 11

Washington

In January 1969 President Richard Nixon and the 91st Congress were sworn into office.

The inauguration was an exciting time for Shirley. Congressman Adam Clayton Powell came over to kiss her hand as she entered the House of Representatives, and outgoing President Lyndon B. Johnson was photographed giving her a bear hug at an evening dance.

Shirley paid for a chartered bus so that her friends and neighbors from Bedford-Stuyvesant could share the historic occasion with her.

In addition to Shirley, two other new black congressmen were sworn into office. Louis Stokes of Cleveland, Ohio, and William Clay of St. Louis, Missouri, became the first black men of their states to join the House of Representatives. That brought the number of Negro representatives in Congress to nine. As *Ebony* magazine put it, nine black members in the House of Representatives was hardly an explosion of political power, but nevertheless, it was a real gain.*

Shirley's first weeks in Washington were hectic as she adjusted to her new schedule. Like the other congressmen from New York, Shirley flew back and forth on the airline shuttle, arriving in Washington on Sunday night and returning to her Brooklyn home on Thursday evening. Since she had traveled to Albany every week for her work in the State Assembly, the long-distance commuting was familiar to her.

The reporters in Washington were just as eager for interviews with the first black congresswoman as the reporters in New York had been. Shirley tried to limit her interviews to one a day, but she wasn't always successful —the reporters never gave up.

One of the newspaper headlines that she really enjoyed read:

FIRST BLACK WOMAN WILL
"SOCK IT TO" CONGRESS

The television people came up with all sorts of ideas to make each interview with Shirley Chisholm a little different from all the others. One reporter asked if she could film an interview with Shirley while the first black congresswoman was standing in the kitchen and doing

* See note 5, page 139

her ironing! After thinking it over, Shirley refused to do that particular interview.

The new congresswoman's office staff could barely keep up with the telephone calls, telegrams, and mail that came into the office every day. The congratulations on Shirley's victory were still pouring in from around the country.

Much of the mail and many of the telephone calls that came into the office turned out to be requests for Shirley's appearance at political meetings and speaking engagements. Many of the requests were from high schools and colleges. Shirley found those requests hard to refuse. Soon her engagement calendar was booked solid for the entire year!

During her first weeks in Washington, Representative Chisholm would ask one of the girls in her office to escort her to meetings she had to attend in different parts of the Capitol. She always insisted that she walk back to her congressional office herself. That way she quickly learned how to use the passageways and short cuts between the Capitol office buildings and the House of Representatives without getting lost.

Whenever Shirley walked through the Capitol, she was greeted with a cheery hello and a smile from the secretaries, guards, and maintenance people. Everyone, it seemed, recognized her.

One Sunday evening when Shirley flew back to Washington after a weekend in New York, she had a terrible shock.

When she entered her Washington apartment, she discovered that it had been burglarized in her absence. The thief or thieves had made off with all her clothes—the new knitted suits and coats in pretty pastel colors that she had bought to wear in the House of Representatives.

Shirley called the police to report the burglary. She also made plans to move to a new address. The following day two reporters found out about the theft and broke the story in the afternoon papers.

That brought a whole new group of reporters to her office looking for more facts about the burglary. Everything that happened to Shirley Chisholm was considered important news.

Shirley decided she had better things to talk about to newspaper men than the theft of her Washington wardrobe.

"Everything I have to say I've already reported to the police," she said firmly. "Some of my friends are going to help me select new clothes and they're going to be prettier than the ones that were stolen."

That finished the matter as far as Shirley Chisholm was concerned. She kept her new address and telephone number out of the newspapers.

One of the speaking engagements that Shirley accepted with pleasure was the Delta Sigma Theta sorority—an organization of Negro college graduates and professional women.

At a luncheon meeting of Delta held at the Americana Hotel in New York, Shirley was initiated into the sorority. Then she gave her speech.

"Everyone in Washington tells me I'm just a freshman congressman, and you're supposed to keep quiet as a freshman," she told the women. "I listen sweetly to them and then I say, 'Thank you for your advice, gentlemen.' But when I get up there on the floor of Congress, I'm sure you'll understand that I'm speaking with the pent-up emotions of the community!"

The audience applauded her warmly, and Shirley went on, "One thing the people in New York and Washington are afraid of in Shirley Chisholm is *her mouth!*"

Shirley's speech that day proved to be prophetic. When she returned to Washington the following Monday, she found herself involved in her first congressional fight.

Shirley and the other freshmen Democrats had been patiently waiting for their committee assignments. Congress is run by the committee system, and unless a congressman is put on a good committee, there is little he— or she—can contribute in the way of legislation.

Shirley understood the importance of getting on a

good committee because of her experience in the State Legislature in Albany, where her position on the Education committee had helped to pass the SEEK legislation.

There were several committees in Congress that she thought she would like to serve on—committees to which she thought she could make an important contribution.

Several black residents of the city of Washington urged her to try for an appointment to the House Committee on the District of Columbia. The District Committee watched over the affairs of the city of Washington, and since 60 per cent of Washington's population is black, a black legislator on the District Committee would have a great understanding of the problems and needs of Washington.

But Shirley had her heart set on the House Education and Labor Committee. Her background in the field of education—the many years she spent as an administrator of New York's child care program and her experience on the Education committee in the State Legislature—were excellent qualifications for the Education and Labor Committee of the House of Representatives. Besides, Shirley told herself, if she were put on the Education committee, she could work for a national SEEK program similar to the one she had helped to put forward in New York State.

Shirley's new friends in Congress told her that her chances of getting on the Education committee were very slim. Education was an important and powerful committee. The positions on it generally went to congressmen who had been in Washington for many years.

That was the meaning of "seniority"—a word Shirley heard often in Washington. The best committee assignments went to members of Congress with seniority—and the congressmen with the most seniority, Shirley discovered, were the Southerners, many of whom had served in Washington for more than twenty years.

Shirley was undaunted. She wrote a letter to the chairman of the Education committee outlining her qualifications and experience. She concluded her letter by respectfully requesting that she be considered for a spot on the committee.

"Maybe if I explain it to them very nicely," she told Conrad, "they'll make an exception to the seniority practice and give me the assignment."

Shirley received a short note of reply from the Education committee's chairman. It said that her letter had been received and it thanked her for her interest.

But Shirley soon learned where the power lay. Representative Wilbur Mills of Arkansas, the chairman of the House Ways and Means Committee, was the man who assigned his fellow Democrats to the various committees.

Mills decided to ignore the wishes of the nation's first black congresswoman. He put Shirley Chisholm on a House Agriculture subcommittee on Forestry and Rural Villages.

"Can you imagine that?" Shirley sputtered to Conrad when she heard the news. "Forestry and Rural Villages! What has *that* got to do with Bedford-Stuyvesant? I guess all the gentlemen in Washington know about Brooklyn is that a tree once grew there."

Shirley was hurt and upset. She talked over her bad luck on the committee assignment with some other freshmen congressmen from the New York delegation. They hadn't done much better, but they didn't care to make a fight over it.

The more Shirley thought about it, however, the angrier she became. "I was elected to Congress from an urban area," she said to Conrad. "I don't know anything about forestry. Besides, nothing I do on the forestry subcommittee is going to help the problems of the cities. I'm going to ask for a change in assignment."

Shirley went to the Speaker of the House of Representatives, John McCormack of Massachusetts, and asked for a transfer to another committee. McCormack listened kindly to her but refused to help.

"Why don't you accept the assignment and be a good soldier, Mrs. Chisholm," the House Speaker said to her. McCormack was in his eighties and he had been in Washington a long, long time.

Shirley thought over McCormack's advice. "No," she said to herself. "That's what's wrong with the country. There are too many 'good soldiers' accepting too many bad decisions."

At the next full meeting of the House Democratic caucus, Shirley asked that the caucus withdraw her name from the House Agriculture subcommittee.

Wilbur Mills was astonished. No one had ever bucked his authority before.

"Will the gentlewoman from Brooklyn withdraw her request?" Mills asked.

Shirley shook her head. If Mills thought he was going to call her bluff, she had to prove to him that she wasn't bluffing. It was a tough moment for a freshman congresswoman. The caucus was silent as the black congresswoman from Brooklyn and the senior congressman from Arkansas both refused to budge.

The caucus didn't vote on Shirley's request. But a few weeks later, the unheard-of happened. Shirley Chisholm got a change of assignment! Mills placed Shirley on the Veterans Affairs Committee.

"At least," Shirley told reporters, "there are veterans in

Brooklyn. And there is a Veterans Administration Hospital there too. I can see where I can contribute something on the Veterans Affairs Committee. I intend to use my position on this committee to see to it that all veterans are informed of their rights and benefits under the law."

One reporter wrote that Shirley Chisholm's battle over her committee assignment was the most vivid sign of life to date in the 91st Congress.

Shirley's run-in with the senior members of Congress didn't lessen her outspokenness one bit. "I am particularly struck by the number of aged men who represent America," she told one interviewer. "It seems we are not taking into consideration what is happening in this country today. We are not giving bright young people—who are often so much in touch with the times—a sufficient chance to break into politics and be heard."

Shirley argued for a change in the seniority system in her public speeches and on television too.

"The rule of seniority in Congress slows down the country's progress," she said on one television program. "It concentrates the power in the hands of a few elderly members who are often too slow to respond to the demands for social change."

Shirley's reputation in Washington as a fearless rebel was established in record time.

CHAPTER 12

Rebel in Congress

The nation's first black congresswoman discovered that she and some of the other liberal members of Congress were thinking along similar lines when it came to legislation. The liberals often got together and asked each other to endorse their bills.

Among the bills to which Representative Chisholm gladly lent her name was a bill to establish a national holiday commemorating the birthday of the slain civil rights leader Martin Luther King.

Representative Chisholm found that there was one area where she found herself in disagreement with many of the other black and liberal congressmen. Many Washington leaders had decided that the answer to the problem of inequality in America lay in the magic words "black capitalism." The way they embraced the new theory made Shirley suspicious.

"Just what is black capitalism?" Shirley argued in her

usual outspoken fashion. "Is it a tax-incentive plan for white businessmen? Just how many black capitalists or businessmen can they create?"

Shirley believed that the way to end poverty in America—for both black and white—was to concentrate on man-power training. "We have to provide jobs for everybody—and train people to fill those jobs," she said time and again.

She wove her theories on the need for a massive man-power training program into her first major speech in Congress.

A huge defense-spending bill related to the war in Vietnam was before the House of Representatives for a vote. Shirley got up to explain to her fellow legislators why she was going to vote no:

"I am going to vote against *this* defense money bill and *every* defense money bill that comes before the House of Representatives until the time comes when our values and priorities have been turned right side up again," Shirley told the other members of Congress.

"As I take this stand today I am joined by every mother, wife, and widow in this land who ever asked herself why the generals can play with billions while families crumble under the weight of sickness, hunger, and unemployment."

Shirley's powerful first speech to Congress came three

months after her inauguration. It was one more proof that the little black lady from Brooklyn was not satisfied with merely being *in* Congress but that she intended to make her voice heard on all the major issues of the day.

Shirley became honorary president of the National Association for Repeal of Abortion Laws (NARAL), which seeks to have the laws making abortion a crime abolished, laws that Shirley Chisholm has called "cruel, inhuman and archaic" (old-fashioned).

National and international issues were exciting—but Shirley didn't forget about the 12th Congressional District in Brooklyn that she was elected to represent.

After searching for a long time for the right location, Shirley opened a Congressional District Office in the heart of the district on Eastern Parkway. During the week—when Shirley was in Washington—the Brooklyn office was run by Wesley Holder and a staff of young people that he and Shirley had selected. Every Friday evening, Congresswoman Chisholm sat in a large back room in the Congressional District Office and met with her constituents—the neighborhood people from the 12th Congressional District.

These Friday evenings in the Brooklyn District Office were an important part of Shirley's life as a congresswoman. The people who came to see her each week had problems that they hoped their representative in Congress would help them solve. Some of the people who came to see Shirley were trying to get into a public housing project, some were trying to get into work training programs, some were having trouble with the Welfare Department or with their landlords. Often a telephone call or letter from Representative Chisholm could straighten the matter out.

The Firday evenings were also important to Shirley because it was a good opportunity for her to discuss politics with the people who had helped elect her. As a sensitive congresswoman she knew that she always needed to be in touch with what the people in her district were thinking about a variety of issues.

During Shirley's first year in Congress, it was time for the New York City mayoral elections. Mayor John Lindsay, who had served the city for four years during a tough period of school strikes, garbage strikes, and subway, bus, and taxi strikes, was running for re-election, but he was being challenged by someone in his own Republican Party. The Democrats put up several candidates for their own Democratic Party primary.

Shirley's choice in the Democratic primary didn't win. Mayor Lindsay was beaten by his fellow Republican in his own primary. The newspapers were calling the results of both primaries a victory for conservatism and white backlash.

Mayor Lindsay was on the ballot for the general election in November as an independent candidate and as the candidate of the Liberal Party. He called Representative Chisholm and asked her for her support.

Shirley thought it over. She decided that Lindsay was the best candidate in the race—and that as an honest politician, she *had* to support him regardless of party labels.

Shirley announced her support of Mayor Lindsay at a press conference at City Hall. She was the first Democratic representative to join the mayor's campaign openly.

The reaction within the Democratic Party was predictable. Shirley's fellow Democratic congressman from Brooklyn, the eighty-one-year-old Emanuel Celler, declared on television that he thought Representative Chisholm ought to resign her post as Democratic National Committeewoman! Other Democrats joined with Celler to attack Shirley Chisholm for breaking party ranks.

"This is just a further indication to me," Shirley answered back, "that some party leaders are not attuned to what is happening in this country."

As usual, Shirley weathered the storm. The rebel congresswoman didn't resign her seat on the Democratic National Committee. *The Amsterdam News* took to calling her a black Joan of Arc. Lindsay was re-elected.

It was a Saturday evening and Shirley and Conrad had decided to spend it quietly at home.

"We're not going to answer the telephone at all," Shirley said to Conrad. "It's only going to be some reporter wanting a statement from me on one thing or another."

The Chisholms were in the kitchen of their new home on St. John's Place. They were fixing dinner—a special dinner of all the hot and spicy West Indian foods that Shirley and Conrad both loved.

Shirley treasured the quiet moments at home with Conrad. They were such a relief from the frantic pace of her public life. At the house on St. John's Place, Shirley could relax, play the piano, curl up on the sofa and read, or just sit and talk with her husband over a good dinner and a cup of hot tea.

"Well, my first year in Congress certainly hasn't lacked for excitement," Shirley said with a happy sigh. "There's no doubt about it—I've fought some good battles."

"You're leading a fuller life than most people—black or white, male or female," Conrad said, smiling in agreement. "I knew when I married you that Shirley Chisholm was going to make a name for herself."

"You know," Shirley said, "I've been thinking lately about all the people who encouraged me to make something of my life—Granny Seales on the farm who taught me about hard work, my mother and father who wanted me to go to college more than anything in the world, and Professor Warsoff at Brooklyn College who was the first person to suggest that I go into politics for a career. And then there were the three heroines that I used to read about—Harriet Tubman, Susan B. Anthony and Mary McLeod Bethune. Their life stories encouraged me, too, by proving to me that it could be done."

"Don't you think that your life story will encourage the young people who are growing up now?" Conrad asked.

Shirley didn't answer. She didn't have to. Her smile said it all. She was very, very happy.

Some Facts You Might Like to Know

1. In the State Assembly a bill is first discussed by a small committee. A new bill to do with housing would be discussed by the Housing committee, a bill on schools by the Education committee, and so on. Although thousands of bills are introduced each year to the State Assembly only a small number gets past this committee stage and on to the floor of the Assembly. When a bill does get "reported out," it is then voted on by all the assemblymen. If the bill is approved by the Assembly it goes on to the State Senate. If it is approved by the Senate, it goes on to the governor of the state. If the *governor* doesn't like the bill he can veto it—that is, he can refuse to sign it so that it cannot become law.

2. Lobbyists work for all the various interest groups that want certain bills passed or defeated in the Legislature (such varied groups as the Teamsters Union, the

State Harness Racing Association, the American Medical Association, the Civil Liberties Union, the NAACP—to name a very few). The lobbyist's job is to persuade the assemblymen and senators of their organization's point of view with statistics and arguments. They are known as lobbyists because years ago they used to do most of their work in the lobby outside the legislative chamber.

3. The legislative branch of the national government was divided by our Founding Fathers into the Senate and the House of Representatives. The purpose of the Senate was to give equal voice in Washington to each of the *states*. Whether the state is large or small, there are two senators to represent it in the United States Senate.

The House of Representatives, however, was set up to give equal voice to the people of the nation on a *population* basis. The number of representatives—or congressmen—each state is allowed is determined by the number of *people* within the state. Furthermore, the Constitution goes on, each district represented by a congressman should be as close as possible in population size to every other congressional district.

The Supreme Court took notice that some congressmen in Washington represented districts that were lightly populated while other congressmen represented districts that were very heavily populated. The Supreme Court's famous "one man, one vote" doctrine of the early 1960s was an important message to the states of the union. It was the Court's way of reminding the nation that according to the Constitution every individual American was entitled to equal representation in the lower chamber of Congress—the House of Representatives.

4. Election rolls are the official lists of people who are registered voters in a particular district.

5. In the nineteenth century, during the Reconstruction period after the Civil War, seven black men sat in Congress.

Three black freshmen congressmen joined the House in 1968 to make a total of nine. The other six are: Adam Clayton Powell of New York (first elected in 1944), eighty-two-year-old William L. Dawson of Chicago (elected in 1942), Charles Diggs of Detroit (elected in 1954), Robert Nix of Philadelphia (elected in 1958), Augustus Hawkins of the Watts district in Los Angeles (elected in 1962), and John Conyers of Detroit (elected in 1964). Until Shirley Chisholm's victory, fewer than one hundred white women had been elected to Congress since 1789—the year of the first United States Congress in history—and no black women at all.